Saskatchewan's Communities in the 21st Century: From Places to Regions

Saskatchewan's Communities in the 21st Century: From Places to Regions

Jack C. Stabler
and
M. Rose Olfert

Canadian Plains Research Center, 2002

Copyright © 2002 Canadian Plains Research Center, University of Regina

Copyright Notice

All rights reserved. No part of this work covered by the copyrights hereon may be reproduced or used in any form or by any means — graphic, electronic, or mechanical — without the prior written permission of the publisher. Any request for photocopying, recording, taping, or placement in information storage and retrieval systems of any sort shall be directed to the Canadian Reprography Collective.

Canadian Plains Research Center
University of Regina
Regina, Saskatchewan S4S 0A2
Canada
Tel: (306) 585-4795
Fax: (306) 585-4699
e-mail: canadian.plains@uregina.ca
http://www.cprc.ca

National Library of Canada Cataloguing in Publication Data

Stabler, J.C., 1935-
 Saskatchewan's communities in the 21st century

(Canadian plains reports, ISSN 0384-8930 ; no. 11)
Includes bibliographical references and index.
ISBN 0-88977-147-2

1. Saskatchewan--Rural conditions. 2. Municipal government--Saskatchewan.
3. Saskatchewan--Economic conditions--1945-1991. 4. Saskatchewan--Economic conditions--1991- I. Olfert, M. R. (Margaret Rose), 1950- II. University of Regina. Canadian Plains Research Center. III. Title. IV. Series.
HN110.S35S72 2002   320.8'097124   C2002-910947-7

Cover Design: Donna Achtzehner, Canadian Plains Research Center

Printed and bound in Canada by Houghton Boston, Saskatoon, Saskatchewan

CONTENTS

List of Tables vi
List of Figures vii
Acronyms vii
Preface viii
Acknowledgments x
Chapter 1: The Setting 1
Chapter 2: Central Place Theory 5
Chapter 3: Data Sources and Methodology 9
    Data Sources 9
    Methodology 11
Chapter 4: Trade Centre Evolution 13
    Trade Centre Classification 2001 14
    Communities Reclassified from PSC to FCC Status 19
    Discriminant Analysis 21
    Communities Previously Omitted 22
Chapter 5: Subdivisions Within Functional Levels 25
    Minimum Convenience Centres 25
    Full Convenience Centres 27
Chapter 6: Economic Development and the Mining and Manufacturing Industries ... 29
    The Local Multiplier 30
    Mining and Manufacturing 31
        Mining Communities 32
        Conclusions with Respect to Mining 33
        Manufacturing Communities 34
        Conclusions with Respect to Manufacturing 36
Chapter 7: Infrastructure and Other Considerations 39
    Commuting Patterns 40
    Review of Research on Infrastructure 42
    Infrastructure in Saskatchewan 43
        Highways 43
        Telecommunications 45
        Electricity and Natural Gas 46
        Water 46
        Sewage and Solid Waste Disposal 47
    Local Economic Development Initiatives 48
        Organizations 48
        Methods of Business Development and Retention 49
        Effectiveness 50
        Community Assessment of Development Initiatives 50
    Housing 51
    Conclusion 53
Chapter 8: Functional Economic Areas 55
    Functional Economic Areas 55
        Shopping Patterns 56
        Labour Market Areas 57
        Identifying Functional Economic Areas 57
        Characteristics of the 11-Region System 59
    Conclusions with Respect to FEAs 60
Chapter 9: Conclusions 63
References 67
Appendix: List of Names of All Communities Included in the Study and Their
    1961, 1981, 1990, 1995, and 2001 Status in the Trade Centre Hierarchy 71
Index 83

LIST OF TABLES

Table 1: n-Orders of Functions Provided by m-Levels of Centres 5
Table 2: Estimated Population Required to Sustain Business Activities at Various
 Distances from a Major City 7
Table 3: Populations Required to Support Multiple Establishments in a Community
 Located 150 kilometres from the Nearest Major City 8
Table 4: Functional Classification, Saskatchewan Centres, 1961–1995 13
Table 5: Functional Classification, Saskatchewan Centres, 2001 15
Table 6: Average Number of Businesses of Various Types in Saskatchewan
 Trade Centres, 2001 16
Table 7: Population Distribution of Saskatchewan's Trade Centre System, 2001 18
Table 8: "Top" 46 Communities in Saskatchewan, 2001 18
Table 9: Profiles of Re-Classified and Remaining PSCs, Showing Their Index of
 Functional Strength, 2001 20
Table 10: Discriminant Analysis Classification Results 22
Table 11: Communities Previously Omitted from the Trade Centre Analysis 23
Table 12: Average Number of Trade Centre Functions, Subsets of Communities within
 the MCC Classification, 2001 26
Table 13: Average Number of trade Centre Functions, Subsets of Communities
 within the FCC Classification, 2001 27
Table 14: Full Convenience Centres by Subgroup, 2001 28
Table 15: Own- and Cross-Community, System-Wide, and Level-Specific Impact Multipliers
 in the Trade Centre Hierarchy 30
Table 16: Distribution of Induced Effects (Urban=SWR +PWR) of an Autonomous Expenditure
 Increase 31
Table 17: Experience of Five Small Communities with Substantial Mining Employment 33
Table 18: Experience of MCC, FCC, and PSC Communities with Substantial
 Manufacturing Employment 35
Table 19: Comparison of Communities with Complete Shopping Centre Classification
 in 2001 with 21 Other Centres Classified CSC in 1961 36
Table 20: Commuters to and from Saskatchewan's 46 Major Communities, 1996 41
Table 21: Commuting Statistics by Hierarchy Level in Saskatchewan, 1996 41
Table 22: Highway Access for 46 Saskatchewan Communities by Highway-Type
 Connections 44
Table 23: Telecommunications Services for 46 Saskatchewan Communities by
 Service Type 45
Table 24: Water Sources and Peak Day Flow for 513 Saskatchewan Communities, 2001 47
Table 25: Infrastructure Requirements to Meet Water Quality Standards, Saskatchewan
 Communities, 2001 47
Table 26: Compliance with Solid Waste and Sewage Disposal Regulations in Saskatchewan
 Communities, 2001 48
Table 27: Average Vacancy Rate by City for Private Apartment Buildings of Three
 or More Units, PWR and SWR Centres 52
Table 28: Average Vacancy Rate by Community for Private Apartment Buildings of
 Three or More Units, CSC, PSC and FCC Centres 52
Table 29: Distances Travelled by Rural Dwellers to Shop by Functional Classification
 of Centre, 1991 56
Table 30: Population1 by 11-Region Functional Economic Areas, 1998 .59
Table 31: Commuting Flow Summary–All FEAs, 1996 60

LIST OF FIGURES

Figure 1: Saskatchewan Trade Centres by Functional Hierarchy, 2001 17
Figure 2: Top 46 Communities in Saskatchewan, 2001 40
Figure 3: 11-Region Functional Economic Areas, Saskatchewan 58

ACRONYMS

ATM Automated Teller Machine
CSC Complete Shopping Centre
CSD Census Subdivision
FCC Full Convenience Centre
FEA Functional Economic Area
FTA Free Trade Agreement
GATT General Agreement on Trade and Tariffs
IPSCO Interprovincial Steel and Pipeline Company
LMA Labour Market Area
MCC Minimum Convenience Centre
NAD Northern Administrative District
NAFTA North American Free Trade Agreement
PSC Partial Shopping Centre
PWR Primary Wholesale Retail
RM Rural Municipality
SERM Saskatchewan Environment and Resources Management
SIC Standard Industrial Classification
SWR Secondary Wholesale Retail

PREFACE

Saskatchewan's urban hierarchy, or trade centre system, has been consolidating for several decades. We have studied this process over a 40-year period beginning in 1961, with previous updates for 1981, 1990, and 1995 (Stabler 1986; Stabler, Olfert and Fulton 1992; Stabler and Olfert 1996).

In the present study we update the analysis to 2001. This report is more than an update, however. The previous studies utilized 34 variables to describe each community. For this analysis the set of variables has been expanded to 68. This revision provides a more sensitive and discriminating metric for assessing and classifying communities into functional categories.

This investigation is more inclusive as well. In the previous studies certain types of centres, such as bedroom or resort communities, were excluded from the analysis. In total there were 31 places which had been omitted. The present study has been expanded to include these 31 centres.

The scope of the research has also been expanded. When the initial studies were undertaken, we were aware of additional considerations which influenced the viability of communities and the evolution of the trade centre system, for which we had no data. In the interim we have undertaken numerous complementary analyses which expanded our understanding of the complex process of trade centre evolution. We have incorporated the results of these inquiries in the present study — thus providing a better understanding of how the system functions and how it changes through time.

One of the first of the complementary investigations was an analysis of retail market areas based on a primary survey of shopping patterns of rural dwellers (Stabler and Olfert, 1992). While useful in itself, the information gathered through the identification of shopping patterns helped to make possible two additional related inquiries.

The concept of the multiplier is very useful in economic analysis. The multiplier refers to the change in total income which results from an initial increase in autonomous expenditure. With consumer spending patterns available on a spatial basis it became possible to develop individual multipliers for each level in the hierarchy (Olfert and Stabler 1994). Additional work in this area led to the development of cross-community multipliers (Olfert and Stabler 1999) which made it possible to identify the impact across the entire hierarchy of an expenditure initiated at any level in the system. Thus the spatial impact throughout Saskatchewan, of an investment anywhere in the province, could be estimated. This also permits identification of those communities which have large enough multipliers to retain a major portion of the multiplier impact in the centre and in the regional economy.

Retail shopping patterns also form one of the necessary building blocks for delimiting regional economies. These spatial economies, which we have named Functional Economic Areas are discussed below. The second necessary building block required to define FEAs, is a delineation of labour market areas which were first estimated for 1981 and 1991 (Stabler, Olfert and Greuel 1996) and subsequently updated to 1996. With a current community hierarchy analysis, and with empirically-defined shopping patterns and labour market areas, and spatial multipliers estimated, all of the components required to define FEAs are available.

Before proceeding to a discussion of regions, however, additional topics included in this study which influence community viability, should be noted. One additional body of information that is useful in assessing a community's present status and future prospects consists of the demand thresholds required to support the everyday trade and service activities consumers depend on. The demand threshold refers to the population required to satisfy the sales requirements necessary to support a commercial activity. These were recently estimated for 27 business activities commonly found in rural Saskatchewan (Wensley and Stabler, 1998).

Secondly, apart from the systematic trade centre relationships that influence community viability, non-systematic events such as the establishment of a manufacturing plant or the development of a mine in the immediate vicinity can have an impact on a centre's immediate and future economic prospects. This topic has long been a focus of policy-makers and community development organizations. For this study we have traced the long-term impact of mining and manufacturing development on several Saskatchewan communities over a period of four decades. This analysis makes possible a comparison of the systematic with non-systematic influences on the viability of the individual community, as well as the structural evolution of the trade centre hierarchy itself.

A third topic that has received much attention recently is the relationship between infrastructure and economic development. For this study we have attempted to provide information on selective infrastructure available at various levels in the hierarchy. This is intended to reflect the past investments that have been associated with communities' attainment of different levels in the trade centre hierarchy, as well as to suggest the potential for future development represented by the presence of infrastructure.

All of these different, though related, strands of information are woven together to provide a more complete interpretation of the evolution of the trade centre system than what was previously possible.

Our final exercise is to combine the various community descriptors in order to define the communities of the 21st century—the economic regions or Functional Economic Areas mentioned above.

An FEA is defined as an area that is relatively closed or bounded with respect to the income- producing activities of its residents. It is also relatively closed with respect to a cluster of everyday consumer-oriented business outlets and common public services. Almost all the labour resident in the area is employed in the area and most of the everyday goods and services consumed in the area are purchased within its boundaries.

The delineation of the system of FEAs presented here represents the systematic codification of the activities of Saskatchewan people as they journey to work, shop for goods and services, send their children to school, access public infrastructure and go about their everyday lives. Their activities define the functional communities of today and for the future.

The body of the study which follows discusses first the setting—how we got to where we are. We then review the conceptual framework, identify data sources and explain the methodology utilized. The 1961–95 classifications are summarized and the 2001 classification is explored in detail and evaluated in the context of past trends. Other influences, particularly mining, manufacturing and infrastructure are then discussed. The emergence of regional economies—the communities of the 21st century— is then discussed in detail. Our conclusions follow.

ACKNOWLEDGEMENTS

This study was funded by Saskatchewan Agriculture and Food and Saskatchewan Economic and Co-operative Development.

Capable research assistance was provided by Darren Barber, Blaine van Melle and Clint Dobson.

CHAPTER 1

The Setting

The year 1870 marks a significant turning point in the history of the prairie region. In that year title to this region passed to the newly created Dominion government, bringing to a close two centuries of control by the Hudson's Bay Company.

At the time of the transfer the region was very sparsely populated. There were but 73,000 persons recorded by the Census taken in 1871—56,000 Aboriginals and 17,000 non-Aboriginals (Urquhart and Buckley 1965).

The transfer of title from the Hudson's Bay Company to the Dominion government resulted in a complete change of policy regarding the use of the area. While the Company had attempted to protect the wilderness character of the region, the government's objective was to create an economically prosperous commercial union of the former British colonies and territories in the northern half of North America.

The government's attempt to stimulate the settlement of the Prairies was implemented through several distinct, but interrelated, programs: generous land disposal schemes (1872); the building of a transcontinental railroad (completed in 1885); treaties with Aboriginal inhabitants (1871–77); protective tariffs (1879); and the 1897 Crow's Nest Pass Agreement establishing low freight rates "in perpetuity" (Fowke 1957).

The response to the government's development initiatives was very modest during the 1880s and 1890s. The price of wheat, the region's major potential export, fell continuously throughout the last third of the 19th century. Although there was general deflation following the American Civil War, wheat prices declined more rapidly than the general price level from the mid-1880s (Urquhart and Buckley 1965).

The situation changed following 1897. Due to a rapid increase in urbanization in Britain, continental Europe and eastern North America, the trend in wheat prices was continuously upward for the next 20 years. Homestead entries followed and between 1900 and 1904 more entries than in the preceding quarter century were recorded in the Prairie region (Urquhart and Buckley 1965; Martin and Morton 1938; MacIntosh 1934).

During the first three decades of the 20th century Saskatchewan was Canada's fastest growing province. Between 1900 and 1930, there were 303,000 homestead entries in Saskatchewan. The territory that became the province of Saskatchewan in 1905 saw its population increase from 91,000 in 1901 to 922,000 in 1931. During this interval the number of farms grew from 13,000 to 136,000.

The railways that were built to carry the region's staple products to world markets provided lines within 16 kilometres of virtually every farm. When the system had reached its point of maximum expansion in Saskatchewan, farmers could deliver their grain to points spaced at an average distance of only 12 kilometres. Other types of businesses serving the farm trade were encouraged to locate at the grain stops and through this process, the number of communities in Saskatchewan eventually reached 906 (Hodge 1965). The establishment of the "Wheat Province" was complete.

Even as the settlement of the Prairies was nearing completion, however, technological advances were being made that would render obsolete the system that was being built. Only the Depression of the 1930s and World War II postponed the inevitable secular adjustment that otherwise would have begun just as the settlement phase ended.

The 1930s saw a complete reversal of Saskatchewan's previous experience: drought, falling grain prices, out-migration, farm consolidation, the beginning of rural-to-urban migration, and the decline of rural communities. Saskatchewan's population fell by more than 100,000 during the 1930s and 1940s.

With the end of World War II, the adoption and implementation of new technologies accelerated during the 1940s and have continued to the present with only occasional and temporary interruptions. By emphasizing mechanization in place of more labour-intensive processes, these new technologies dramatically affected the organization of activities conducted in rural settings and, consequently, the communities that served rural industries and consumers. Particularly important in this respect were the developments that facilitated the substitution of capital for labour in agriculture, thus making it possible for fewer farmers to produce the same, or even a growing, volume of output (Britnell 1939; Barger and Landsberg 1942; Phillips 1956; Fowke 1957). Another factor contributing to the consolidation of agricultural holdings in the Prairie region was the quota system, under which the amount of grain that could be delivered for marketing was based on the number of acres farmed rather than output per acre. Farmers were therefore encouraged—both by technological progress and by marketing policies set by the Canadian Wheat Board— to expand their land base (Furtan and Lee 1977).

Transportation, communications, and distribution activities were also affected by the development of new technologies. In the 1950s, for example, an ambitious program to update Saskatchewan's intercity road network was initiated. As a result, paved intercity roads increased from 1,200 to 16,000 kilometres between 1951 and 1971; all-weather, connecting gravel road mileage increased fourfold during the same interval (Saskatchewan Department of Highways records).

One of the first reorganizations to follow the improvement in road access was that of the rural school system. Between 1951 and 1971, some 2,750 schools in rural areas and small communities were closed (Saskatchewan Department of Education records). Elementary school students were bused into nearby communities, while high school students travelled to regional high schools that were developed in larger, locally central communities.

Reorganization of the postal and rural telephone systems came next. Between the mid-1950s and 1980, 390 rural post offices were closed and 322 local telephone offices were converted from manual to dial exchanges (Canada Post and SaskTel personal communications September 1995). These reorganizations and consolidations eliminated many jobs in rural areas and small communities, and transferred others to intermediate-sized or large urban communities (Stabler 1986). The beginning of economic diversification and growth of major urban centres led to a reversal of the province's population decline. Between 1951 and 1961, Saskatchewan regained the 100,000 people lost during the 1930s and the 1940s. By 1961, the population had reached 925,000.

The rural trade centre system adapted to these changes. Smaller communities declined while the larger, centrally located rural communities prospered, at least initially, from the consolidation process and expanded. Rural dwellers, both as consumers and producers, contributed to the pattern of concentration. As paved roads were extended into all regions of the province, shopping patterns shifted from the closest rural community to regional shopping centres where more stores, greater variety, and sometimes better quality and lower prices were available. Bypassing of intermediate-sized communities became common, and in response, new commercial development increasingly occurred in the larger centres as it withered away in the small communities (Stabler and Williams 1973). In a study of Saskatchewan's trade centre system between 1941 and 1961, Hodge (1965) recorded a decline in the number of communities from 906 to 779. Over 150 of the remaining 779 had populations of fewer than 50.

Although the relative importance of specific influences affecting the structure of Saskatchewan's space-economy differed from one decade to the next, for many years the sequence was complementary. That is, as the intensity of one influence diminished, another took its place, and so it has gone for approximately five decades.

For the most part, the adjustments of the 1950s, 1960s, and 1970s were conducted within a generally prosperous environment. Prices received for Saskatchewan's basic commodities did fluctuate, of course; in some years, poor harvests coincided with low prices, but periods of prosperity followed. The mid-to-late 1980s were different, however. World overproduction of small grains, coupled with the failure of GATT to restore order in international grain markets, resulted in several successive years in which prices received were at or below the cost of production. Farm incomes were supported by a series of federal and federal-provincial relief and income support programs and an increasing number of farm families took permanent off-farm jobs.

In the 1960s and 1970s, trade centre decline was concentrated in smaller communities. In the 1980s and 1990s, it reached much higher into the urban system, and only a few large, diversified, and centrally located rural communities escaped its consequences.

The long period of economic growth in the North American economy throughout most of the 1990s had a positive effect on most sectors of the provincial and national economies. Grain farming has been the exception. The brief upturn in grain prices in the early 1990s was followed by a return to world overproduction, falling prices and the maintenance of, or return to, massive subsidies by the European Union and the United States.

Canada has largely withdrawn from the subsidy war, however. The small annual deficits incurred by federal and provincial governments into the 1970s turned, in the 1980s, into a haemorrhage of such proportions that it threatened fiscal disaster. Consequently, the unconditional transfers to the agricultural sector have been replaced with much leaner safety nets financed out of contributions by both levels of senior government and by producers as well. Further, the federal government's termination of the Crow Rate, which subsidized the movement of grain to export positions, has resulted in a substantial increase in the cost of shipping grain. For producers in the more remote areas of Saskatchewan, termination of the Crow subsidy has reduced net farm income by two-thirds (Stabler and Olfert 1999). Restructuring of the agricultural sector away from grain farming is underway.

In other areas, lower levels of transfers from federal to provincial governments, in conjunction with a concerted effort to bring deficits under control, have resulted in reduced transfers by the provincial government to municipalities and reduced spending on health, education, welfare, and transportation, as well as on agriculture. Since many of these expenditures were directly for infrastructure, the provincial budget was balanced at the cost of the infrastructure eroding away. There is now in Saskatchewan a multibillion dollar backlog of infrastructure requirements.

Saskatchewan has come to a crossroads as it enters the 21st century. It will not be possible to simultaneously reduce taxes (or even maintain them at present levels), balance the budget, and replace or repair the entire complement of the province's infrastructure. It is very likely that the future configuration of the province's infrastructure will differ markedly from that of the past.

Finally, the World Trade Organization, successor to GATT, which continues to promise to reduce agricultural subsidies, is part of a broader framework of much freer trade across all sectors, with FTA and NAFTA being the most prominent. Because of the emphasis on much greater efficiency the opportunities for cross-subsidization, which cushioned adjustments in past decades, have been greatly reduced. Businesses in most sectors of the economy will now have to meet the competition of firms not only in the next town or the next province, but from around the world.

The remainder of this study is devoted to an analysis of the evolution of Saskatchewan's trade centre system into the 21st century. We discuss the conceptual framework, data sources and methodology, and provide an analysis of changes, and then give our summary and conclusions.

CHAPTER 2

Central Place Theory

Central place theory is the theory most widely used to explain the number, size, and spacing of centres in a system of urban places. According to this theory, the role of the central place is to act as a service and distribution centre for its hinterland, providing its own, and the adjacent, population with goods and services. Why such functions are provided from central places is explained by the concepts of the demand threshold and the range of the good. The threshold is defined in terms of the minimum level of population and income required to support a particular activity, while the range refers to the maximum area that the activity in question can serve from a particular place. The range is limited because transport costs raise the price of the item as distance from the central place increases. This is true regardless of whether the item is a good distributed from the centre or is one that customers have to travel to the centre to obtain.

Table 1
n-Orders of Functions Provided by m-Levels of Centres

Order of Function	Level of Centre					
	Lowest	m-4	m-3	m-2	m-1	m
n						x
n-1					x	x
n-2				x	x	x
n-3			x	x	x	x
n-4		x	x	x	x	x
lowest	x	x	x	x	x	x

Since the threshold and range will differ among various activities, a hierarchical spatial structure results in which the activity with the lowest threshold requirement is found in all central places. In today's context, a gasoline service station would typify a service function with a low demand threshold. Only a small population is required to provide the level of demand necessary to support a gasoline station. Therefore, many exist and they are distributed widely — wherever a small concentration of population is found. Activities requiring a larger threshold, however, are found in fewer and larger places. Since the size of service areas varies directly with the size of centres, the complementary regions of small places are contained within those of larger places. Table 1 illustrates how n-orders of functions are provided by m-levels of centres.

The required number of functions of each type, and thus the number of centres of each size within the system, is largely a function of total population and income, while the spacing of centres is determined by population density and accessibility. Higher incomes and larger populations are associated with a greater number of functions. Although the number of centres is directly related to population density, it is inversely related to the quality of the region's transportation systems.

Referring to Table 1, it is apparent that the lowest level of centre would provide only the lowest-order function. The next largest community, m-4, would also provide the lowest order function to its own and the immediately adjacent rural population. But the larger community also offers the next highest-order function, n-4. These services are provided to its own residents plus the population contained within several adjacent centres of the lowest level and all of the rural population contained within this larger market area. Each successively higher-order function, offered from increasingly higher-level centres, is provided to all lower-level centres and the rural populations within the ever-larger market areas of the higher-order functions. Often, several functions will have approximately the same demand threshold and a similar range. Thus, the number of functions of any given order will typically be greater than the single function implied in Table 1.

Where the individual community is situated relative to the largest centres in the system also influences the size of the demand threshold required to support each function. Most Saskatchewan residents make some consumption expenditures in one or more of the province's 10 largest centres. The closer they live to one of these larger places, the more often they will visit them. Thus the closer a smaller community is to one of the province's major centres, the greater the population required to support any type of function.

Some results from a recent study of demand thresholds for a variety of functions at different distances from the province's 10 largest communities are reported in Table 2 (Wensley and Stabler 1998).

Populations reported in Table 2 are community populations associated with the presence of the functions identified. Since approximately 30 percent of the province's population lives outside any community, the actual populations required to support the functions named would be approximately 30 percent larger than the figures appearing in the table.

Activities with low demand thresholds identify the more common types of businesses frequently present in smaller communities: restaurant, grocery store, gas station, hotel (beverage room). Activities with higher demand thresholds are associated with businesses usually found in larger rather than smaller centres: furniture stores, drug stores, automobile sales.

The functions in Table 2 are arrayed in ascending order of population required to support a single outlet at a distance of 150 kilometres from one of the province's 10 largest communities. The fact that the entries in the other distance columns do not increase monotonically indicates that some functions are more sensitive than others to competition from similar businesses in larger places.

Activities less sensitive to competition from larger places include gas stations, construction firms (often local craftsmen), and restaurants. Such activities are characterized as local market-area dependent functions.

Activities producing products or services which are characterized by less frequent purchases, greater differentiation, and higher expenditures per sale are more likely to be affected by competition from a larger city. Thus clothing stores, home furnishings, and automobile sales are classified as regional market-area dependent functions. For these activities the population required to support one outlet at 25 kilometres from a major centre is approximately twice that required at 150 kilometres. For the local market area-dependent activities previously named, the difference is only 25–30 percent.

Table 2
Estimated Population Required to Sustain Business Activities at Various Distances from a Major City

Business Activity	Distances from the Nearest City (km.)			
	25	50	100	150[a]
Construction	295	270	250	235
Hotel	515	395	305	265
Bank	670	505	380	320
Gasoline Station	505	465	435	415
Credit Agency	550	495	445	420
General Store	955	700	515	430
Grocery Store	640	550	475	435
Bulk Fuel	1005	750	555	470
Restaurant	685	615	555	520
Building Materials	825	705	605	550
Farm Equipment	1045	845	685	605
Transportation	1055	850	690	610
Wholesale	1045	870	720	645
Clothing Store	1505	1155	890	765
Special Credit	1140	995	870	805
Auto Repair	1185	1025	890	815
Miscellaneous Repair	1410	1235	1080	1000
Automobile Sales	2190	1675	1285	1100
Home Furnishings	1995	1590	1265	1110
Special Foods	1825	1560	1335	1220
Drugstore	1875	1695	1530	1445
Recreation	3635	2730	2055	1735
Business Services	2150	2165	2180	2190
Furniture Store	3100	2790	2460	2295
Personal Services	3360	2920	2540	2340
Warehousing	3860	3545	3260	3100
Laundry[b]	—	—	4645	3870

[a]Ranked in ascending order of population requirements at 150 kilometres
[b]Population estimate greater than largest community population in sample

In Table 3, the community populations required to support multiple outlets of the selected functions, at 150 kilometres from a major centre, are identified. Activities offering relatively homogeneous products or services display constant or increasing population increments to support additional outlets in the same community. Hotels, farm equipment dealers, general stores, grocery stores, gas stations, banks (and credit unions), and auto repair shops fall into this category. Activities offering more differentiated products or services, such as clothing stores, home furnishings stores, automobile dealerships, and business services, are associated with decreasing population increments required to support additional outlets.

Distortions from the theoretical model occur in response to several common phenomena. Rugged topography or uneven resource distribution, for example, leads to uneven population distribution and to transport networks that provide better access to some areas than others. Further, the theory provides a better explanation of the functioning of centres in agricultural than in highly industrialized regions. The service centre role is more clearly apparent when there are few places of large size in a region. When there are several large centres of similar size, there is a greater possibility of specialization by function, such as manufacturing or government, for example, which may lead to a distortion of the urban size hierarchy.

In spite of these qualifications, the theory is the most useful one available for the analysis of trade centre systems. No other theory stresses so much the fundamental interdependence of the community and the region within which it is located. Further, at the operational level, the specific theoretical relationships are capable of empirical verification.

Central place theory is well suited for the topic at hand. Saskatchewan's economy

Table 3
Populations Required to Support Multiple Establishments in a Community Located 150 kilometres from the Nearest Major City

Business Activity	Number of Establishments			
	1	2	3	4
Construction	235	455	675	890
Hotel	265	645	1095	1590
Bank	320	845	1490	2225
Gasoline Station	415	910	1440	1995
Credit Agency	420	790	1150	1500
General Store	430	1280	2435	3835
Grocery Store	435	910	1405	1915
Bulk Fuel	470	1130	1900	2745
Restaurant	520	950	1360	1745
Building Materials	550	940	1385	1825
Farm Equipment	605	1215	1830	2445
Transportation	610	1290	2000	2735
Wholesale	645	1270	1895	2520
Clothing Store	765	1180	1530	1835
Special Credit	805	1280	1675	2030
Auto Repair	815	1640	2465	3295
Miscellaneous Repair	1000	1975	2945	3910
Automobile Sales	1100	1875	2570	3215
Home Furnishings	1110	1765	2320	2820
Special Foods	1220	2160	3025	3840
Drugstore	1445	2405	3250	4020
Recreation	1735	2880	3875	4795
Business Services	2190	3435	4470	5390
Furniture Store	2295	3645	4780	5795
Personal Services	2340	3575	4565	5470
Warehousing[a]	3100	5125	—	—
Laundry[a]	3870	5910	—	—

[a] Population estimate greater than largest community population in sample

was initially based on agriculture, and this sector still provides the basis for much of the employment and income generated within the province. The majority of Saskatchewan's communities came into existence to serve the needs of the agricultural economy. Indeed, their locations were determined primarily by the transportation requirements of the grain industry, and many Saskatchewan communities still perform an agricultural trade centre function. In addition, there are no really large cities in the province. The largest, Saskatoon and Regina, have specialized to an extent, but both still are dominant communities in the province's trade centre system.

Central place theory describes a system in equilibrium, that is, one in which population size and distribution, income, and technology are unchanging. Because of this property, it is referred to as a static, general equilibrium theory, which might at first appear as a drawback given the significant changes in technology, income, and the distribution of the province's population over the past several decades. The apparent limitations of a static theory are circumvented to a degree by performing what is referred to as comparative static analysis, whereby the characteristics of the system are completely identified at two points in time. In a dynamic economy, the system would be expected to differ at dates separated by several years. These differences then become the focus of attention, and an effort is made to interpret and explain the changes noted by reference to evolving technologies, improvements in transportation, rising incomes, and the behaviour of people as both consumers and producers, as well as to other influences that may become apparent in the conduct of the analysis. (A thorough discussion of central place theory is available in Berry and Parr 1988).

CHAPTER 3

Data Sources and Methodology

This study of Saskatchewan's trade centre hierarchy extends to 2001 the analysis of this system conducted at four previous dates over the past 40 years. The present study maintains continuity with the past by focussing on the 598 communities that were the object of the four previous analyses. The present endeavour differs from those of the past by developing classifications for several communities which, for one reason or another, were previously excluded. For continuity, the discussion focusses on the 598 places. A discussion of the (mostly small, special purpose) communities previously excluded is provided separately.

In addition, the number of variables used to describe the commercial, industrial, and public structure of communities was refined and expanded for the 2001 study. The revised set of variables will produce a more sensitive, improved classification of the communities that form the trade centre system. Because it is not *identical* to the data set used in previous studies, however, the 2001 classification is not *precisely* comparable to those of the past. If the old data set had been used for the present study, it is possible that the outcomes would have been slightly different. Similarly if the present data set had been used for the 1995 study, the results would have been more precise. It is possible that those results would have been somewhat different.

Data Sources

The communities included in this analysis are those 598 incorporated and unincorporated places that, in 1961, had 50 or more inhabitants *and* were listed in the 1981 census. The structure of the trade centre system was analyzed at four previous dates: 1961, 1981, 1990 and 1995. Each of these studies included the same 598 places, employed the same data set, and utilized the same methodology. The present study includes the same 598 communities and employs the same methodology. As previously noted, however, an expanded and refined set of variables is used for this analysis.

Data describing each community were collected from a variety of sources. Information on the number of business outlets in the communities was purchased from Dun & Bradstreet which maintains a data base listing businesses according to individual Standard Industrial Classification (SIC) codes, by community.

In all previous studies the businesses were grouped into 29 categories. For the present study an expanded list of 59 individual business functions was used to describe the commercial and industrial structure of communities. The expanded set was created, in the first instance, by listing separately some functions that were previously combined. For example, laundries and dry cleaners which were previously combined were identified separately for 2001. This provides for greater discrimination among communities since dry cleaners require a larger population to support them than do laundries. Secondly, some functions such as computer stores and ATMs, which appeared after 1961 (and were consequently never individually identified in the variable set), were added for the present study. In another refinement, three separate categories of services to business management (Services to Primary Producers, Professional Business Services, and Other Business Services) replaced a single category (Business Services) used in the earlier studies. In this case the revision reflects the fact that this function has become much more important in the economy since 1961 and therefore needed to be included in greater detail in the 2001 profiles. The number of lawyers was added as a variable for the first time.

Yet another revision replaced variables previously recorded as either "present or absent" with a quantitative measurement. Thus high school enrollment (grades 10, 11, and 12) at schools in each community replaced an indicator of the presence or absence of a high school (and elementary schools were included for the first time, also by way of enrollment in elementary grades K through 9). Health care facilities were represented this time by four variables (instead of the former two—presence or absence of hospitals and special care homes) to reflect the major changes that have occurred in this sector. For two new variables, Clinics and Health Centres, simple presence or absence was indicated. The number of rated beds was used to represent Hospitals (acute care and respite) and Special Care Homes (long term care). Where long term beds were present in Health Centres, the community was identified as both having a Health Centre and having the indicated number of beds in a "Special Care Home." The Grain Elevator variable (previously presence or absence) was represented by the total number of deliveries (tonnes) at that point.

In all, 68 variables were used to describe the functional structure of communities in the present study, replacing the 34 previously utilized. No variable used in the previous studies was omitted, though several were disaggregated and refined units of measurement were developed for several others. In addition, several variables not previously utilized were added for the present study as noted above. These modifications, additions, and refinements provide a more sensitive and discriminating metric for assessing and classifying communities into functional categories within the trade centre hierarchy.

Data used for all variables were 2000 or 2001 values with one exception. It was necessary to use the 1996 census for population counts. In previous studies the "Covered Population" from Saskatchewan Health was utilized. The Covered Population data for 1997 and earlier were based on the Health Insurance Registration File, and for 1998 onward has been based on the Person Registry System. The two systems are different in the way in which geographic location is assigned. Since 1998, the geographic location of individuals is identified either by a Residence Code (optionally provided), or the Community in the mailing address (always available). For rural residents, their mailing address will always identify some community even though they do not live in the community. If they do not also (voluntarily) identify their residence, they are automatically allocated to the community. Even where they do identify their residence, "corrections" are sometimes made at Sask Health assigning the community in the mailing address as the Residence Code. Because of these changes in the way individuals are geographically located, it was not possible to use Saskatchewan Health Covered Population for the 2001 population. To do so would have greatly distorted the actual spatial distribution of the population, especially in rural areas and small communities.

Methodology

In order to group the communities in the study into functional categories, a cluster analysis program was utilized. Cluster analysis is a classificatory technique designed to select subsets of mutually similar objects from the set of all such objects. In this case, the task is to select subsets of functionally similar communities from the entire set of 598 communities. Each community is described by a comprehensive set of attributes, all of which are considered simultaneously in the classification scheme. The relevant quantifiable characteristics of a community include population size, the entire array of business functions, and the additional infrastructure as described under Data Sources in the preceding section. Through a complex computer algorithm, the program is able to evaluate, compare, and ultimately group centres on the basis of their similarities in terms of the dimensions in which they are described.

For the cluster analysis, the raw data were standardized prior to clustering. A similarity matrix was subsequently computed where the coefficients represent the distance between communities. Clusters were formed using Ward's method, which minimizes the distance between the subject and its group centroid as fusion proceeds.

After formation of the clusters, they were tested for compactness and distinctness using multiple discriminant analysis. In all cases the groups were found to be statistically valid.

This technique resulted in the formation of six distinct clusters. Given the theoretical context for the analysis (Central Place Theory), these six clusters are taken to represent the functional categories in a trade centre hierarchy. These categories are commonly described as Minimum Convenience Centre (MCC), Full Convenience Centre (FCC), Partial Shopping Centre (PSC), Complete Shopping Centre (CSC), Secondary Wholesale-Retail (SWR), and Primary Wholesale-Retail (PWR).

Minimum Convenience Centres are the smallest, and functionally simplest, trade centres, offering a small, though eclectic, set of services such as perhaps a gasoline station or a restaurant, functions that require a relatively small-sized market area. In addition, a limited number of less frequently used goods or services is occasionally available. In the next tier are Full Convenience Centres, which typically offer a set of goods and services that require a somewhat larger-sized market area, such as groceries and banking services. Communities in each subsequent tier in the hierarchy (Partial Shopping, Complete Shopping, Secondary Wholesale-Retail, and Primary Wholesale-Retail) perform all of the functions of the centres in the previous tiers and, in addition, offer more sophisticated goods and services that require larger market areas. The particular functions performed at each tier will vary over time and from one geographic area to the next, but the hierarchical structure of trade centres will persist because of the differential market areas required to support a complete array of goods and services.

CHAPTER 4

Trade Centre Evolution

We begin by comparing the number of communities in each functional classification for 1961, 1981, 1990, and 1995. These comparisons are provided in Table 4. Between 1961 and 1981, a very substantial downward movement of communities in the middle categories occurred.

Table 4
Functional Classification, Saskatchewan Centres, 1961–95

Functional Classification	1961	1981	1990	1995
Primary Wholesale-Retail (PWR)	2	2	2	2
Secondary Wholesale-Retail (SWR)	8	8	8	8
Complete Shopping Centre (CSC)	29	22	6	7
Partial Shopping Centre (PSC)	99	30	46	22
Full Convenience Centre (FCC)	189	136	117	59
Minimum Convenience Centre (MCC)	271	400	419	500
Total	598	598	598	598

In 1961, for example, there were 317 communities situated in the three clusters between the Secondary Wholesale-Retail (SWR) level and the lowest functional classification, the Minimum Convenience Centre (MCC). By 1981, the number occupying this interval had decreased to 188. During this time period, the number of communities in the Complete Shopping Centre (CSC) category decreased by only seven (25 percent), but the Partial Shopping Centre (PSC) and the Full Convenience Centre (FCC) categories experienced much greater downward movement.

Between 1981 and 1990 there was some further downward movement of centres in the middle categories, but at a much slower rate. The number of communities in the three clusters below the SWR and above the MCC levels declined from 188 in 1981 to 169 in 1990. What is most striking about the 1981–90 period is the pronounced decline of communities that had held CSC status in 1981—only 6 of 22 centres (27 percent) remained in this category in 1990.

In the 1990–95 period, there was again a very substantial downward reclassification of communities in the middle categories. The number of centres between the SWR and the MCC levels decreased to 88. Thus, over the 34 years between 1961 and 1995, middle-level communities decreased from 53 to 15 percent of the total, while the number of centres in the bottom (residual) category, MCC, increased from 45 to 84 percent.

The interval between 1990 and 1995 was again characterized by stability at the top three functional levels; indeed, there was one addition to the CSC category. The most striking feature of the 1990–95 period, however, was the dramatic downward reclassification of the communities that had occupied the PSC and FCC categories in 1990: 50 percent of the 1990 PSCs and 70 percent of FCCs had moved to a lower classification by 1995.

Over the interval between 1961 and 1995, the experience of communities below the Secondary Wholesale-Retail category (in 1961) was commonly a gradual downward filtering through a number of stages. Most communities classified as Complete Shopping Centre, or below, in 1961, first gradually filtered to the bottom of the functional category they were originally observed in. They were subsequently reclassified downward where they became the top communities in their new category. As more time passed, they slowly descended to the bottom of their new functional category and were eventually again reclassified to the next lower level.

At the top of the hierarchy, the 10 Wholesale-Retail centres retained their status throughout the 1961–95 period. In addition, six communities classified as Complete Shopping Centres in 1961 retained their status over the entire interval. A seventh, Melville, began as a CSC, declined to PSC in 1990, and regained CSC status in 1995. These 17 communities grew substantially in population as well as in the number and variety of businesses and infrastructure over the 34-year period ending in 1995.

Below the CSC level, downward reclassification was the common experience although five of the original 99 PSCs did retain their status between 1961 and 1995. Of the 22 communities classified as PSCs in 1995, most had declined into that category between 1961 and 1981.

Trade Centre Classification 2001

At the top three levels of the hierarchy, the 2001 classification is almost identical to that of 1995. Saskatoon and Regina retain their dominant positions as the two PWR centres and the same eight secondary cities continue to occupy the SWR classification.

The Complete Shopping Centre category includes the seven communities classified at this level in 1995 (Humboldt, Kindersley, Meadow Lake, Melfort, Melville, Nipawin, and Tisdale). There has been one addition at this level, however. Assiniboia, which was a CSC between 1961 and 1981, but declined to PSC in 1990, regained CSC status in 2001.

At the bottom of the hierarchy, the 1995 and 2001 classifications contain virtually the same number of communities (502 in 2001 and 500 in 1995), although the specific communities included differ slightly. The number of centres between the SWR and MCC levels declined slightly from 88 to 86 in 2001.[1]

The major difference between the 2001 and 1995 classifications occurs at the PSC and FCC levels. While there were 22 PSCs and 59 FCCs in 1995, the 2001 classification contains only six PSCs, while the FCC category has increased to 72. Of the 22 communities classified as PSCs in 1995, one (Assiniboia) rose to CSC status, six retained their PSC classification and 15 were reclassified as FCCs. The functional classification for 2001 is shown in Table 5.

The overall structure of the system and the pattern of change observed—continued downward reclassification of middle-level communities—between 1995 and 2001 is consistent with the historical evolution of the hierarchy.

The 2001 profiles of the six functional classifications, provided in Table 6, indicate the role played by communities at each level. The 10 communities in the Primary and Secondary Wholesale-Retail functional classifications are distinguished from

---

1. Between 1995 and 2001, 15 communities rose from the MCC to FCC status while 17 declined from FCC to MCC.

Table 5
Functional Classification, Saskatchewan Centres, 2001

Primary Wholesale-Retail (PWR)	2
Secondary Wholesale-Retail (SWR)	8
Complete Shopping Centre (CSC)	8
Partial Shopping Centre (PSC)	6
Full Convenience Centre (FCC)	72
Minimum Convenience Centre (MCC)	502
Total	598

those in the bottom four in several ways. They provide multiple outlets of a complete range of consumer and producer services. They also have a greater variety and concentration of manufacturing and construction activity. Their health and educational facilities are more numerous, larger and more specialized.

At the top end, the major distinction between the PWR and SWR categories is the depth and variety of functions. PWR centres, for example, have 5 to 10 times the number of consumer and producer services firms of each type per community than the SWR centres. Therefore PWR centres offer the greatest range in variety, quality and price. The producing sector (manufacturing and construction) is, likewise, much larger in PWR centres with from 10 to 30 times as many firms per community as SWR centres. Health and education facilities and services are also much more numerous and varied at the PWR level.

In distinguishing between SWR and CSC communities, the hierarchical structure of the system starts to become very explicit. While most common consumer services are provided at the CSC level, a few high-order functions, such as camera stores, dry cleaners, department stores, and security brokers are much less common. The common presence of these functions at the SWR, but not the CSC, level is indicated by the block of numbers in italics, bold, and underlined that extends between the SWR and the CSC columns in Table 6.[2] With respect to Producer Services, the major difference between these two levels is in the greater number of firms (in total and of each type) per community in SWR centres. In the Producing sector, a major distinction does become apparent, however. Manufacturing activity at the CSC level (and lower) is concentrated in basic resource processing, as well as fabricating and assembly types of activities. While Primary and Secondary Wholesale-Retail centres also engage in these basic types of manufacturing, they are (almost exclusively) home to most of the province's intermediate-stage manufacturers and producers of final consumer goods—activities which are less common in centres below the SWR level. In health and education functions the difference between CSC and SWR levels is number and size rather than presence or absence. Although the 8 CSC centres are overshadowed by communities in the SWR category, they are nevertheless the largest and most viable of the province's rural communities.

Complete and Partial Shopping Centres differ less in terms of functional distinctiveness than in number of outlets per function. Nevertheless, some higher-order consumer services (shoe stores and laundries) are common at the CSC but not the PSC levels. In addition, air transportation, common at the CSC level, is almost totally absent at lower levels. Again, in terms of manufacturing and construction activity, CSC communities have, on average, a much larger number of firms than PSCs. A similar comment can be made about health and education where the number and size of functions is larger in CSC communities.

---

2. In comparing the average number of functions in the major categories (bold print in column headings in Table 6) for 2001 with our 1995 study, a substantial increase is apparent. This is explained by the fact that we have included more variables for the 2001 study. In addition, the years between 1995 and early 2000 saw considerable growth in the economy during which time there was a substantial increase in the number of business firms.

Table 6
Average Number of Businesses of Various Types in Saskatchewan Trade Centres, 2001

Count	502	72	6	8	8	2
Functional Classification	Minimum Convenience	Full Convenience	Partial Shopping	Complete Shopping	Secondary Wholesale-Retail	Primary Wholesale-Retail
Population	168	1,083	2,233	4,364	18,361	187,024
All Consumer Services	5.65	36.89	101.82	131.70	392.71	3,181.50
Luggage	0.00	0.01	0.00	0.00	0.50	*5.00*
Camera Stores	0.00	0.01	0.17	0.50	*0.88*	6.00
Dry Cleaning	0.00	0.04	0.00	0.38	*1.13*	21.50
Department Stores	0.00	0.11	0.33	0.50	*2.00*	7.50
Security Brokers	0.00	0.18	0.17	0.25	*2.88*	34.00
Laundries	0.01	0.08	0.50	*0.88*	4.63	30.50
Shoe Stores	0.00	0.11	0.33	*1.13*	2.25	22.50
Furniture Stores	0.01	0.22	*1.00*	1.38	4.63	32.50
Credit Agencies	0.16	0.76	*1.17*	1.50	2.50	27.00
Electronics Outlets	0.04	0.33	*1.33*	3.25	6.63	48.50
Jewellery Stores[1]	0.00	0.15	*1.67*	0.75	1.75	16.50
Building Materials	0.09	0.72	*1.67*	1.88	6.75	29.50
General Merchandise	0.24	0.81	*1.67*	2.63	3.25	14.00
Drug Stores	0.04	0.86	*1.83*	1.75	3.88	37.50
Other Personal Services	0.03	0.85	*1.83*	2.25	11.13	77.00
Other Food Stores	0.11	0.82	*1.83*	5.25	7.38	83.50
Lawyers	0.01	0.40	*2.50*	7.00	24.00	208.50
ATMs	0.01	0.78	*2.67*	4.63	15.75	147.00
Floor/Drap./Appliances	0.03	0.58	*2.83*	5.63	13.38	85.00
Apparel Stores	0.02	*0.90*	3.50	5.38	11.88	128.50
Beauty/Barber Shops	0.06	*0.90*	3.83	1.50	13.13	139.00
Insurance Agents	0.22	*1.01*	2.17	2.88	8.25	106.50
Hardware Stores	0.18	*1.24*	2.50	3.38	5.88	27.50
Hotels	0.32	*1.28*	4.67	3.38	10.38	39.50
Recreation	0.17	*1.32*	4.50	5.25	15.38	158.00
Service Stations	0.34	*1.47*	2.83	3.00	10.00	69.50
Banks or Credit Unions	0.38	*1.79*	3.17	3.88	8.13	58.00
Misc. Retail	0.26	*1.89*	3.50	7.75	23.13	178.50
Grocery Stores	0.38	*1.99*	4.00	3.50	13.00	87.50
Automobile Dealers	0.13	*2.10*	5.83	7.63	19.75	108.00
Eating and Drinking	0.43	*2.19*	7.33	7.75	28.50	325.00
Misc. Repair	0.19	*2.93*	9.33	11.13	40.00	347.00
Auto Repair	0.31	*3.00*	8.83	10.25	29.50	241.50
Real Estate Agents	*1.48*	5.06	12.33	13.50	40.50	234.00
All Producer Services	2.08	13.08	30.51	38.91	153.78	1688.50
Warehousing	0.03	0.32	0.83	*0.88*	4.38	36.00
Air Transportation	0.00	0.06	0.00	*1.13*	2.00	6.50
Professional Bus. Serv.	0.06	0.58	*1.17*	3.38	17.88	385.50
Bulk Fuel	0.23	0.85	*1.67*	1.50	2.38	5.00
Communic./Utilities	0.02	0.35	*2.17*	1.63	7.38	58.00
Other Business Services	0.10	*0.89*	2.67	3.88	25.25	348.50
Implement Dealers	0.15	*1.06*	4.83	2.63	6.00	24.00
Bus. Serv. to Primary	0.34	*2.29*	6.17	5.13	21.63	79.00
Transportation	0.29	*2.29*	4.17	5.50	23.88	165.50
Other Wholesale	0.86	*4.39*	6.83	13.25	43.00	580.50
Grain Deliveries[2]	*10.60*	62.92	153.80	217.43	333.63	410.10
All Producers	0.97	7.97	17.67	30.03	97.27	994.50
Leather Manufacturing	0.00	0.06	0.33	0.00	0.00	*3.00*
Textiles Manufacturing	0.00	0.07	0.00	0.00	0.13	*6.00*
Furniture/Fixtures Mfg.	0.01	0.03	0.00	0.25	0.25	*15.50*
Paper Manufacturing	0.00	0.00	0.00	0.25	*1.00*	4.50
Apparel Manufacturing	0.01	0.03	0.50	0.38	*1.00*	16.50
Electrical/Instruments	0.01	0.03	0.17	0.38	*1.25*	35.00
Chem/Petro/ Mfg	0.03	0.19	0.17	0.63	*2.25*	44.50
Misc. Manufacturing	0.01	0.15	0.67	0.50	*2.38*	34.50
Stone/Concrete Mfg.	0.02	0.38	0.50	*1.25*	3.25	23.50
Lumber/Wood Mfg.	0.06	0.39	0.67	*1.50*	5.25	30.00
Food Manufacturing	0.06	0.33	0.83	*1.88*	2.88	39.50
Pri. Metal/Metal Fab.	0.03	0.21	*1.00*	1.38	3.50	46.50
Printing	0.02	0.56	*1.33*	2.00	5.13	63.50
Equipment Mfg.	0.10	0.65	*1.67*	3.13	6.25	55.50
Construction	0.61	*4.89*	9.83	16.50	62.75	576.50
Public Infrastructure						
Clinics[3]	0.01	0.03	0.00	0.13	0.38	*1.00*
Health Centres[3]	0.06	0.39	0.00	0.00	0.00	0.50
Doctors[4]	0.06	*1.51*	2.67	7.00	33.5	503.50
Hospital Beds	0.14	*7.74*	20.50	38.50	103.88	742.00
Special Care Beds	*1.55*	34.83	49.33	93.00	206.88	1,372.50
HS Enrollment	*12.78*	94.29	186.83	317.00	1,212.25	9,174.00
ES Enrollment	*42.44*	263.11	487.00	885.75	3,230.13	26,839.00

[1] This is the only function that meets the threshold at one level and not at a higher.
[2] Grain deliveries, unlike other functions in this group, refers to the volume of business rather than the number of business outlets.
[3] For this variable the presence or absence of the function is measured.
[4] Where a doctor is present for one day a week, for example, this is counted as .20.

Chapter 4: Trade Centre Evolution

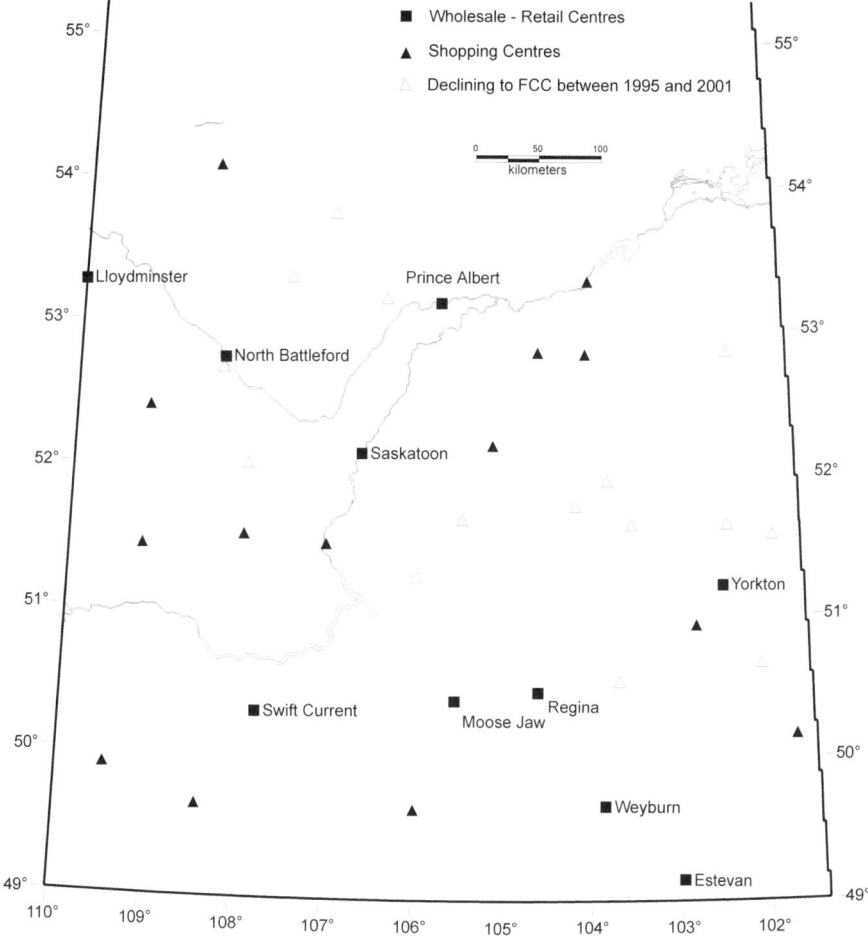

Figure 1: Saskatchewan Trade Centres by Functional Hierarchy, 2001.

There is a very substantial difference between PSC and FCC classifications, however. FCCs do not provide a full range of consumer services. Rather they typically provide only one to two outlets of each of the most basic consumer services—food, gasoline, banking, minor repair—while PSCs provide multiple outlets of these basic services plus a dozen or so more specialized services. A large block of consumer services shown in italics-bold-underlined ranging from Furniture Stores to ATMs first appear with regularity at the PSC level. Similarly, while several producer services are present, the high-tech professional business services (management consultants, engineers, architects, accountants, etc.) firms are uncommon at the FCC level. Manufacturing is largely absent as well in FCC communities, although construction firms are still common. Health and education functions have become fewer and smaller. The average statistics of 1.5 doctors and a hospital with 7.74 beds reflect the fact that these services are not available in all FCC communities. In fact only 85 percent of FCC centres have any level of local access to a doctor (even a one-day-a-week presence is counted as the availability of this service), while only 44 percent of FCC communities have a hospital. Nevertheless, most FCCs continue to perform a locally useful function in the provision of several day-to-day requirements.

Table 7
Population Distribution of Saskatchewan's Trade Centre System

Functional Classification	Centres			Population		
	No.	%	cum. %	No.	%	cum. %
PWR	2	0.33	0.33	374,047	51.12	51.12
SWR	8	1.34	1.67	146,885	20.08	71.20
CSC	8	1.34	3.01	34,908	4.77	75.97
PSC	6	1.00	4.01	13,396	1.83	77.80
FCC	72	12.04	16.05	77,957	10.66	88.46
MCC	502	83.95	100.00	84,416	11.54	100.00
Total	598	100.00		731,609	100.00	

Table 8
"Top" 46 Communities in Saskatchewan, 2001

Strongest Full Convenience Centres	Partial Shopping Centres	Complete Shopping Centres	Secondary Wholesale-Retail	Primary Wholesale-Retail
Battleford	Maple Creek	Assiniboia	Estevan	Regina
Big River	Moosomin	Humboldt	Lloydminster	Saskatoon
Biggar	Outlook	Kindersley	Moose Jaw	
Canora	Rosetown	Meadow Lake	North Battleford	
Carlyle	Shaunavon	Melfort	Prince Albert	
Davidson	Unity	Melville	Swift Current	
Esterhazy		Nipawin	Weyburn	
Fort Qu'Appelle		Tisdale	Yorkton	
Hudson Bay				
Indian Head				
Kamsack				
Kipling				
Leader				
Lumsden				
Maidstone				
Oxbow				
Redvers				
Shellbrook				
Spiritwood				
Wadena				
Watrous				
Wynyard				

Finally, the 502 communities in the MCC category, as a group, no longer perform a coherent role in the trade centre network. There is no single function that can be counted on to be present in each of these places. While the average MCC will have approximately six consumer outlets, they consist of an eclectic combination of functions that vary from place to place. Infrastructure is largely absent and only the occasional producer or producer service outlet is found in communities at this level. Figure 1 is a map of the 2001 trade centre hierarchy.

An additional summary perspective of the province's trade centre system is shown in Table 7 where the total population of the communities that comprise the hierarchy is allocated to the six functional levels. These statistics indicate, perhaps even more forcefully than the preceding discussion, the importance of the centres in the top functional classifications. The 10 communities in the Wholesale-Retail categories account

Chapter 4: Trade Centre Evolution

for less than 2 percent of the system's trade centres but over 70 percent of its population. The 574 places in the bottom two functional categories account for 96 percent of the communities but only 22 percent of the population.

In Table 8, the names of the 24 communities that presently occupy the top four functional classifications are listed along with those 22 that were classified in the top group of FCCs when this group was clustered separately.[3] Included in this group of 22 FCCs are 14 of the 15 communities that were reclassified from PSC to FCC status and eight comparable FCCs in terms of population, business structure and public infrastructure (as identified in the separate cluster analysis). Foam Lake, the fifteenth community reclassified from PSC to FCC, was not included in the top tier of the FCCs. Since the reclassification of communities from PSC to FCC status represents the most significant structural change observed in the interval since the last trade centre study, some attention to detail is provided in the following section.

Communities Reclassified from PSC to FCC Status

In 2001, 15 communities that had been classified as Partial Shopping Centres in 1995 were reclassified to FCC status. Although these 15 centres have profiles which are "strong," relative to the majority of other communities in the FCC classification they are smaller and functionally "weaker" than the six places that retained PSC status.

In Table 9 the profiles of the 15 reclassified centres is compared with those of the six retaining their PSC classification. An "index of functional strength" is also provided showing the value of the variable in question for the 15 relative to the six. Thus for Banks or Credit Unions, for example, the average of 2.00 for the group of 15 is divided by the average of 3.17 for the six. The result of 0.63 indicates that the 15 have approximately two-thirds as many outlets per community for this function as do the six.

Another way to compare the 15 with the six is by noting that the average population size of the 15 reclassified centres is 83 percent that of the six. Thus in any instance where the index of functional strength is less than 0.83, the 15 will have not only a lower absolute strength than the six but also a lower per capita strength. Looked at in this way, the 15 centres that were reclassified have individual functional strength indices which equal or exceed 0.83 in only seven of the 57 possible comparisons. Thus while the 15 continue to play a locally important role in the trade centre system, the six communities retaining PSC status are functionally stronger communities.

All smaller rural communities are, of course, affected by the continuous exodus of rural population and by the gradual geographic expansion of rural labour markets. Loss of population reduces the support for local business, particularly the higher order functions which distinguish PSCs from FCCs. Geographic expansion of the labour market area increases competition in the job market and sometimes results in fewer local people working in the local retail sector or at the mine, mill or factory. Commuters from distant locations will shop in communities closer to where they live rather than where they work, thus reducing support for the community which is associated with the employment site, even though employment may be stable or even growing.

Location within the hierarchy is also a factor in a community's economic evolution. Many of the centres that were reclassified are within the retail market area of a larger place. For example, Shellbrook near Prince Albert, Indian Head near Regina,

---
3. See Chapter 5 below for a discussion of the clustering of FCC communities.

Table 9
Profiles of Re-Classified and Remaining PSCs, Showing Their Index of Functional Strength, 2001

			Index of
Count	15	6	
Status	Declining	Stable	Functional Strength
Population	1,850.67	2232.67	0.83
All Consumer Services	51.87	101.83	0.51
Luggage Stores	0.07	0.00	—
Camera Stores	0.07	0.17	0.40
Dry Cleaning	0.07	0.00	—
Department Stores	0.20	0.33	0.60
Security/Commodity Brokers	0.13	0.17	0.80
Shoe Stores	0.20	0.33	0.60
Laundries	0.00	0.50	—
Jewellery Stores	0.60	1.67	0.36
Furniture Stores	0.40	1.00	0.40
Drug Stores	1.07	1.83	0.58
Credit Agencies	0.80	1.17	0.69
Electronics Stores	0.67	1.33	0.50
Building Materials	1.27	1.67	0.76
General Merchandise	1.00	1.67	0.60
Other Personal Services	1.40	1.83	0.76
Other Food Stores	1.27	1.83	0.69
Floor/Draperies/Appliances	0.73	2.83	0.26
Lawyers	1.27	2.50	0.51
ATMs	1.60	2.67	0.60
Hardware Stores	1.40	2.50	0.56
Hotels	1.53	4.67	0.33
Insurance Agents	0.93	2.17	0.43
Apparel Stores	1.67	3.50	0.48
Beauty/Barber Shops	0.87	3.83	0.23
Service Stations	1.80	2.83	0.64
Banks or Credit Unions	2.00	3.17	0.63
Grocery Stores	2.80	4.00	0.70
Automobile Dealers	3.40	5.83	0.58
Recreation	1.93	4.50	0.43
Miscellaneous Retail	4.33	9.33	0.46
Auto Repair	3.87	8.83	0.44
Eating and Drinking	3.07	7.33	0.42
Miscellaneous Repair	3.00	3.50	0.86
Real Estate Agents	6.47	12.33	0.52
All Producer Services	16.67	30.5	0.55
Air Transportation	0.13	0.00	—
Warehousing	0.33	0.83	0.40
Bulk Fuel	0.93	1.67	0.56
Communication/Utilities	0.53	2.17	0.25
Professional Business Services	0.67	1.17	0.57
Implement Dealers	1.40	4.83	0.29
Business Services to Primary	2.27	6.17	0.37
Transportation	3.07	4.17	0.74
Other Business Services	1.80	2.67	0.68
Other Wholesale	5.53	6.83	0.81
Grain Deliveries	96.86	153.80	0.63
Producers	12.07	17.67	0.68
Leather Manufacturing	0.07	0.33	0.20
Textiles Manufacturing	0.13	0.00	—
Furniture/Fixtures Manufacturing	0.07	0.00	—
Paper Manufacturing	0.00	0.00	—
Apparel Manufacturing	0.07	0.50	0.13
Electrical Manufacturing	0.00	0.17	—
Miscellaneous Manufacturing	0.27	0.67	0.40
Chem/Petro/Rubber Manufacturing	0.40	0.17	2.40
Stone/Concrete Manufacturing	0.73	0.50	1.47
Lumber and Wood Manufacturing	0.60	0.67	0.90
Food Manufacturing	0.67	0.83	0.80
Pri. Metal/Metal Fabrication	0.53	1.00	0.53
Printing	0.73	1.33	0.55
Machinery/Transp. Equipment	0.80	1.67	0.48
Construction	7.00	9.83	0.71
Public Infrastructure			
Clinics	0.07	0.00	—
Health Centres	0.00	0.00	—
Doctors	2.53	2.67	0.95
Hospitals	16.27	20.50	0.79
Special Care Homes	53.27	49.33	1.08
High School Enrolment	129.60	186.83	0.69
Elementary School Enrolment	402.47	487.00	0.83

Biggar and Watrous within Saskatoon's retail market area, and Davidson between Regina and Saskatoon. In these circumstances, competition from the larger centre(s) prevents the development or hinders the retention of those higher-order functions that distinguish the PSC from the FCC category.

In a different circumstance, some of the declining PSCs were one of a cluster of adjacent communities of equal status. For example, Wynyard, Wadena, and Foam Lake, and Canora and Kamsack were all classified as PSCs in 1995. Mutual competition among essentially similar communities for a market that could not support all the centres at the same level contributed to the decline of all to FCC status. In the case of Battleford, although legally a separate community, it is economically inseparable from North Battleford and its reclassification has little economic significance.

Yet another set of influences is associated with the resource-based economies of Big River, Esterhazy, and Hudson Bay. In all resource/extractive industries technological change continues to result in the substitution of capital for labour. This reduces the amount of employment required to produce a given level of output. There has also been a trend in recent years to contract out work that was previously done internally (within the firm). Contractors may be from other communities. There is also some economic incentive to replace several small local contractors with fewer, larger contractors who may also operate out of larger centres where they have access to a larger market.

Returning to locational considerations, the communities retaining PSC status are characterized by larger populations and by locations well removed from a centre of a higher level. The six centres retaining their PSC classification have an average population 21 percent larger than the 15 that were reclassified. These communities—Moosomin, Shaunavon, Rosetown, Maple Creek, Outlook, and Unity—are all approximately an hour's drive from a higher level centre. Larger size and greater isolation facilitate the retention or development of multiple outlets of those functions that distinguish the PSC from the FCC level.

Spiritwood is a community reclassified from PSC to FCC that does not fit readily into the explanations already offered for a reduction in level. Spiritwood is located in a mixed livestock-grain producing area, well removed from either Prince Albert or North Battleford. Its isolation has facilitated the development and retention of a complement of consumer services that greatly exceeds what would be common for a community of approximately 1,000. In fact, in terms of presence of consumer functions, Spiritwood compares favourably with the six centres that retained the PSC classification though its smaller population cannot support the multiple outlets common to the six. Spiritwood also has a strong complement of producer services, especially those that support the agricultural industry. Again Spiritwood has fewer multiple outlets and about one-third the number of firms in the business services categories as the six centres retaining PSC status. Spiritwood does have a hospital and resident doctors, which is not common for communities of its size. In the producing sector, Spiritwood has about half the number of manufacturing and construction firms that the six centres retaining PSC status have. Spiritwood's strong consumer services and infrastructure ensure it a continuing strong role within its region. Its small population, its relative lack of multiple consumer services outlets, manufacturing and business service firms explain its reclassification.

Discriminant Analysis

The discussion to this point has focussed on the six groups of communities identified with the cluster analysis program, and the characteristics of these groups in terms of the commercial, industrial and public functions they perform. Additional

Table 10
Discriminant Analysis Classification Results

	Group	\multicolumn{6}{c}{Predicted Group Membership}	Total
		PWR	SWR	CSC	PSC	FCC	MCC	
Count	PWR	2	0	0	0	0	0	2
	SWR	0	8	0	0	0	0	8
	CSC	0	0	8	0	0	0	8
	PSC	0	0	0	6	0	0	6
	FCC	0	0	0	0	69	3	72
	MCC	0	0	0	0	6	496	502
%	PWR	100	0	0	0	0	0	100
	SWR	0	100	0	0	0	0	100
	CSC	0	0	100	0	0	0	100
	PSC	0	0	0	100	0	0	100
	FCC	0	0	0	0	95.8	4.2	100
	MCC	0	0	0	0	1.2	98.8	100

98.5% of original grouped cases correctly classified.

insight into the functional grouping of communities within the hierarchy can be obtained by briefly reviewing the results of the discriminant analysis, conducted to test the distinctness and validity of the groups.

In Table 10, the summary discriminant analysis assessment of the grouping achieved with the cluster analysis is provided. The groups defined by the cluster analysis would (if shown) appear on the diagonal with values of 2, 8, 8, 6, 72 and 502 respectively. In Table 10, the group membership predicted by discriminant analysis, based on each community's scores on the five discriminant functions, are recorded. For the top four groups, the assessment is that all communities are correctly assigned. For the 72 communities assigned FCC status in the cluster analysis, 69 are validated in this classification and three were reassigned to MCC status. Of the 502 communities assigned as MCCs in the cluster analysis, 496 were validated while six were reassigned to the FCC category. Overall, 98.5 percent of the originally grouped cases were "correctly" classified.

Actually it is not possible to improve the classification. The communities reassigned in the discriminant analysis are positioned close to the "boundary" of the group to which they were reassigned. But if they are manually moved into the group to which reassignment is indicated, the centroids of both groups change. When the discriminant analysis is then rerun, following the suggested reassignment, a few different communities, near the new boundaries, are indicated for reclassification.

All in all, the six groups of communities are very distinct. Further the groups are quite compact. Only nine communities out of the 598 (1.5 percent) were close enough to the margin of an adjacent group to warrant consideration for reclassification. All of these nine cases were in the two lowest functional categories.

Communities Previously Omitted

In 2001, there were 31 communities with populations of 50 or more which had not been included in any of the previous studies. These places had been excluded in 1961 for a variety of reasons and, consequently, from all subsequent studies as well.

A decision was made at the time of the 1961 study to exclude all communities north of the Northern Administrative District (NAD) boundary as then defined.

It was also decided to exclude all clusters of population which had no (or little) commercial structure. Thus residential suburbs or "bedroom" communities outside of, but adjacent to, Saskatoon and Regina were excluded. In this group were (in order by

Chapter 4: Trade Centre Evolution

Table 11
Communities Previously Omitted from the Trade Centre Analysis

	Type of Community	
Bedroom	Resort/Special Purpose	Trade Centre
Martensville – 3,477	B-Say-Tah – 159	Annaheim – 214
Osler – 618	Beuna Vista – 308	Bjorkdale – 262
Pilot Butte – 1,469	Candle Lake – 463	Bulyea – 99
Warman – 2,839	Caronport – 1,147	Cando – 106
White City – 905	Christopher Lake – 200	Clavet – 339
	Fort San – 265	Fosston – 85
	Katepwa Beach – 103	Hazlet – 120
	Lebret – 226	Makwa – 104
	Sun Valley – 95	McLean – 262
		Middle Lake – 268
		Minton – 101
		Mistatim – 114
		Pierceland – 488
		Pilger – 106
		Sintaluta – 189
		St. Benedict – 119
		Yarbo – 127

current population) Martensville, Warman, Pilot Butte, White City and Osler. All of these communities are characterized by infrastructure and commercial structures which are underdeveloped relative to other centres of similar size situated at greater distances from a major city. Thus Martensville's population, for example, would place it near the bottom of the Complete Shopping Centre category, while its commercial/infrastructure profile would place it in the Full Convenience category. A similar comment would apply to all these bedroom communities. Their populations are relatively large while the number of their commercial/infrastructure functions is small.

Other clusters of population deliberately excluded were communities on Indian Reserves, resort communities such as Katepwa Beach, and special purpose centres such as Caronport (residential Bible School). In all, nine communities were excluded from the intial study under this category. Most of the resort communities have smaller populations, the largest being Candle Lake at 463. The resort communities have a small complement of consumer services but generally no other commercial functions or infrastructure. All would be more like Minimum Convenience Centres than any other classification. Caronport is much larger with a population of 1,147 but its commercial structure is very limited though it does have both an elementary school and a high school.

Another 17 previously excluded places have populations of 50 or more in 2001. One of these, Clavet, had a population of less than 50 in 1961 and was therefore deliberately excluded. The other 16 were excluded for reasons since forgotten, or simply overlooked. All are, or were, conventional trade centres in agricultural areas. The largest of these is Pierceland with a relatively large number of consumer service businesses for a centre of this population. Pierceland's population is similar to that of the largest MCCs while its commercial profile is more like the smaller FCCs. The remaining centres are all smaller and have commercial/infrastructure/population profiles that would place them in the MCC classification. A list of the previously omitted communities, along with their populations is provided in Table 11.

CHAPTER 5

Subdivisions Within Functional Levels

In the 1995 trade centre study the (then) 500 Minimum Convenience Centres were separately reclustered because of the considerable variation within this residual group. Three subsets were identified: 44 larger places with an average population of 499; 201 intermediate-sized places whose average population was 250; and 255 smaller centres with a mean population of 69 residents.

For the present study the 502 MCCs identified in 2001 were again separately reclustered. In addition, the current group of 72 FCCs was also separately reclustered. This category of centres, which was substantially expanded by the reclassification of 15 communities previously classified as PSCs, is also large enough to exhibit considerable internal variation.

Minimum Convenience Centres

The most plausible partitioning of the 2001 group of 502 MCCs produced three subsets whose profiles are shown in Table 12. A group of 72 of the largest places formed the top subset, a group of 123 intermediate-sized MCCs formed the second (middle) subset and the remaining 307 formed the largest group of very small places. Although the group sizes differ noticeably between 1995 and 2001, there is more consistency than first appears. Most of the 44 places in the top category in 1995 are also in the top category in 2001. The same is true of the bottom group. A small number of the middle category moved up into the top category and a larger number descended into the bottom group. In addition, 15 communities rose from the top subset of MCCs to FCC status while 17 declined from FCC to the top tier of MCC communities.

Functionally the three groups are similar in that their commercial structure consists of an eclectic variety of businesses retained from a time when they performed a more clearly defined role in the trade centre system. The statistics in Table 12 indicate that the average community in the subset of 72 largest places retains a semblance of what MCCs once were, offering a service station, a bank or credit union, a grocery store, and an eating and drinking outlet. Even so, the high standard deviations around the means for these functions suggest that two outlets, or none, are about as likely as the average of one. The communities in this group also provide some services to other businesses and will typically house three producers.

The group of 72 largest MCC places has an average population of 437 and houses 31,490 people. This subset includes several relatively remote places whose isolation allows them to continue to perform a few basic services: Cabri, Central Butte, Goodsoil, Kyle, Lucky Lake, Quill Lake. For others in this group, location relative to

Table 12
Average Number of Trade Centre Functions, Subsets of Communities Within the MCC Classification, 2001

Number of Communities	307 smallest		123 middle		72 largest	
Subset						
Population	77.00	83.21	238.11	170.52	437.36	215.90
	Average	Std. Dev.	Average	Std. Dev.	Average	Std. Dev.
All Consumer Services	2.33	6.14	8.30	12.67	15.47	18.24
Luggage Stores	0.00	0.06	0.00	0.00	0.00	0.00
Camera Stores	0.00	0.00	0.00	0.00	0.00	0.00
Dry Cleaning	0.00	0.00	0.00	0.00	0.00	0.00
Department Stores	0.00	0.00	0.00	0.00	0.01	0.12
Security/Commodity Brokers	0.00	0.00	0.00	0.00	0.00	0.00
Shoe Stores	0.00	0.00	0.00	0.00	0.00	0.00
Laundries	0.00	0.00	0.00	0.00	0.08	0.28
Jewellery Stores	0.00	0.00	0.00	0.00	0.00	0.00
Furniture Stores	0.00	0.00	0.03	0.18	0.04	0.20
Drug Stores	0.00	0.00	0.01	0.09	0.26	0.47
Credit Agencies	0.02	0.13	0.33	0.49	0.47	0.53
Electronics Stores	0.00	0.06	0.14	0.37	0.04	0.20
Building Materials	0.02	0.15	0.03	0.18	0.47	0.65
General Merchandise	0.12	0.34	0.30	0.46	0.61	0.70
Other Personal Services	0.00	0.06	0.07	0.28	0.06	0.23
Other Food Stores	0.01	0.11	0.12	0.35	0.53	0.82
Floor/Draperies/Appliances	0.01	0.10	0.01	0.09	0.15	0.40
Lawyers	0.01	0.10	0.00	0.00	0.01	0.12
ATMs	0.00	0.00	0.02	0.15	0.04	0.20
Hardware Stores	0.06	0.24	0.27	0.62	0.56	0.69
Hotels	0.16	0.37	0.54	0.64	0.65	0.81
Insurance Agents	0.05	0.22	0.40	0.60	0.65	0.61
Apparel Stores	0.00	0.06	0.01	0.09	0.10	0.38
Beauty/Barber Shops	0.00	0.00	0.08	0.27	0.31	0.55
Service Stations	0.13	0.39	0.44	0.65	1.11	0.85
Banks or Credit Unions	0.14	0.35	0.59	0.53	1.04	0.64
Grocery Stores	0.11	0.31	0.62	0.71	1.15	0.85
Automobile Dealers	0.06	0.28	0.10	0.35	0.51	0.71
Recreation	0.03	0.20	0.29	0.54	0.56	0.92
Misc. Retail	0.06	0.23	0.24	0.57	0.65	0.95
Auto Repair	0.13	0.38	0.41	0.73	0.90	1.09
Eating and Drinking	0.14	0.36	0.76	0.98	1.13	0.99
Misc. Repair	0.09	0.34	0.46	0.84	0.64	0.91
Real Estate Agents	0.97	1.30	2.04	1.91	2.72	2.37
All Producer Services	1.02	2.70	2.99	5.50	5.03	5.81
Air Transportation	0.00	0.00	0.00	0.00	0.01	0.12
Warehousing	0.00	0.00	0.10	0.30	0.07	0.26
Bulk Fuel	0.13	0.35	0.24	0.50	0.63	0.64
Communication/Utilities	0.00	0.00	0.05	0.22	0.04	0.20
Professional Business Services	0.03	0.20	0.03	0.18	0.19	0.43
Implement Dealers	0.05	0.22	0.22	0.52	0.43	0.62
Business Services to Primary	0.19	0.53	0.52	0.95	0.69	0.87
Transportation	0.09	0.33	0.53	0.90	0.76	0.97
Other Business Services	0.04	0.20	0.20	0.74	0.17	0.38
Other Wholesale	0.49	0.87	1.10	1.20	2.03	1.33
Grain Deliveries	6.70	20.58	13.28	28.46	22.62	26.56
All Producers	0.28	0.95	1.52	3.45	2.93	5.62
Leather Manufacturing	0.00	0.00	0.00	0.00	0.01	0.12
Textiles Manufacturing	0.00	0.00	0.00	0.00	0.00	0.00
Furniture/Fixtures Manufacturing	0.00	0.00	0.00	0.00	0.06	0.23
Paper Manufacturing	0.00	0.00	0.00	0.00	0.00	0.00
Apparel Manufacturing	0.00	0.00	0.00	0.00	0.08	0.33
Electrical Manufacturing	0.00	0.00	0.04	0.24	0.00	0.00
Miscellaneous Manufacturing	0.00	0.00	0.00	0.00	0.10	0.30
Chem/Petro/Rubber Manufacturing	0.00	0.00	0.07	0.29	0.07	0.26
Stone/Concrete Manufacturing	0.00	0.00	0.03	0.18	0.06	0.29
Lumber and Wood Manufacturing	0.00	0.06	0.16	0.47	0.13	0.37
Food Manufacturing	0.00	0.06	0.10	0.35	0.25	0.50
Pri. Metal/Metal Fabrication	0.00	0.00	0.09	0.29	0.04	0.26
Printing	0.00	0.00	0.04	0.20	0.06	0.23
Machinery/Transp. Equipment	0.06	0.26	0.11	0.32	0.28	0.65
Construction	0.22	0.58	0.87	1.12	1.81	2.09
Public Infrastructure						
Clinics	0.00	0.00	0.00	0.00	0.07	0.26
Health Centres	0.00	0.00	0.05	0.22	0.35	0.48
Doctors	0.00	0.01	0.05	0.19	0.35	0.48
Hospital Beds	0.00	0.00	0.00	0.00	0.97	3.34
Special Care Beds	0.00	0.00	0.67	3.79	9.67	13.89
High School Enrolment	2.33	8.90	17.59	32.78	49.14	55.35
Elementary School Enrolment	13.11	32.82	61.88	72.06	134.29	90.09

a larger centre allows them to perform a bedroom service to the larger place: Kenaston, Delisle, Balgonie. And for yet a few others, the presence of manufacturing (St. Brieux) or recreational attraction (Regina Beach) has provided a measure of ongoing support.

For the subset of 123 intermediate and 307 smallest places, there are few businesses of any type and little, if anything, is systematically available. Communities in all three subsets are very much alike in that their health care infrastructure has all but disappeared.

The middle group of 123 places has an average population of 238 and is home to 29,288 residents while the smallest group of 307 places has an average population of 77 and is home to 23,639. In total the 502 MCCs house 84,416 people, between 8 and 9 percent of the province's population. For comparison, the 500 communities classified as MCCs in 1995 claimed a population of 89,804.

Chapter 5: Subdivisions Within Functional Levels

Full Convenience Centres

The 72 communities classified as FCCs in 2001 divide, through the use of cluster analysis, into two distinct groups. First is a group of 22 relatively large centres with an average population of 1,667; the second, a group of 50 with an average population of 825.

Table 13
Average Number of Trade Centre Functions, Subsets of Communities within the FCC Classification, 2001

Number of Communities	50		22	
Subset	smallest		largest	
Population	832.85	315.63	1667.45	727.94
	Average	Std. Dev.	Average	Std. Dev.
All Consumer Services	**30.56**	**26.21**	**51.36**	**36.71**
Luggage Stores	0.00	0.00	0.05	0.21
Camera Stores	0.00	0.00	0.05	0.21
Dry Cleaning	0.00	0.00	0.14	0.35
Department Stores	0.08	0.27	0.18	0.39
Security/Commodity Brokers	0.14	0.40	0.27	0.46
Shoe Stores	0.06	0.24	0.23	0.43
Laundries	0.02	0.14	0.23	0.53
Jewellery Stores	0.00	0.00	0.50	0.51
Furniture Stores	0.16	0.42	0.36	0.58
Drug Stores	0.78	0.58	1.05	0.49
Credit Agencies	0.72	0.45	0.86	0.64
Electronics Stores	0.24	0.48	0.55	0.60
Building Materials	0.54	0.61	1.14	0.77
General Merchandise	0.74	0.85	0.95	0.79
Other Personal Services	0.68	0.87	1.23	1.07
Other Food Stores	0.70	0.76	1.09	0.81
Floor/Draperies/Appliances	0.54	0.79	0.68	0.84
Lawyers	0.16	0.42	0.95	1.17
ATMs	0.42	0.61	1.59	0.80
Hardware Stores	1.08	1.01	1.59	1.05
Hotels	1.18	0.80	1.50	1.10
Insurance Agents	1.00	0.61	1.05	0.49
Apparel Stores	0.60	0.86	1.59	1.26
Beauty/Barber Shops	0.76	0.74	1.23	0.97
Service Stations	1.24	1.04	2.00	1.48
Banks or Credit Unions	1.68	0.59	2.05	0.49
Grocery Stores	1.58	1.14	2.91	1.48
Automobile Dealers	1.56	1.33	3.32	2.50
Recreation	0.90	1.05	2.27	2.07
Misc. Retail	2.28	1.65	4.41	1.99
Auto Repair	2.66	1.57	3.77	1.51
Eating and Drinking	1.88	1.04	2.91	1.48
Misc. Repair	1.52	1.27	2.73	1.72
Real Estate Agents	4.66	3.60	5.95	5.47
All Producer Services	**11.02**	**10.43**	**17.72**	**11.25**
Air Transportation	0.00	0.00	0.18	0.50
Warehousing	0.34	0.52	0.27	0.46
Bulk Fuel	0.72	0.70	1.14	0.77
Communication/Utilities	0.28	0.54	0.50	0.60
Professional Business Services	0.48	0.74	0.82	0.85
Implement Dealers	0.84	0.84	1.55	1.65
Business Services to Primary	2.26	2.66	2.36	1.14
Transportation	1.86	1.47	3.27	2.00
Other Business Services	0.52	0.65	1.73	1.28
Other Wholesale	3.72	2.31	5.91	2.00
Grain Deliveries	57.96	69.38	74.18	79.15
All Producers	**5.40**	**7.09**	**13.77**	**11.23**
Leather Manufacturing	0.04	0.20	0.09	0.29
Textiles Manufacturing	0.02	0.14	0.18	0.39
Furniture/Fixtures Manufacturing	0.00	0.00	0.09	0.29
Paper Manufacturing	0.00	0.00	0.00	0.00
Apparel Manufacturing	0.00	0.00	0.09	0.29
Electrical Manufacturing	0.00	0.00	0.09	0.29
Miscellaneous Manufacturing	0.08	0.27	0.32	0.57
Chem/Petro/Rubber Manufacturing	0.10	0.36	0.41	0.67
Stone/Concrete Manufacturing	0.22	0.46	0.73	0.77
Lumber and Wood Manufacturing	0.24	0.89	0.73	1.08
Food Manufacturing	0.20	0.53	0.64	0.73
Pri. Metal/Metal Fabrication	0.06	0.24	0.55	0.67
Printing	0.48	0.79	0.73	0.55
Machinery/Transp. Equipment	0.58	0.93	0.82	0.80
Construction	3.38	2.27	8.32	3.83
Public Infrastructure				
Clinics	0.02	0.14	0.05	0.21
Health Centres	0.54	0.50	0.05	0.21
Doctors	1.09	0.89	2.55	1.34
Hospital Beds	4.72	8.44	14.59	9.84
Special Care Beds	29.64	18.29	46.64	29.10
High School Enrolment	77.38	33.13	132.73	65.40
Elementary School Enrolment	210.14	75.62	383.50	172.28

Table 14
Full Convenience Centres by Subgroup, 2001

50 Smallest FCCs			22 Largest FCCs	
Balcarres	Ituna	Radville	Battleford	Leader
Carnduff	Kelvington	Raymore	Big River	Lumsden
Carrot River	Kerrobert	Rocanville	Biggar	Maidstone
Coronach	Kinistino	Rockglen	Canora	Oxbow
Cudworth	Lafleche	Rosthern	Carlyle	Redvers
Cut Knife	Lampman	Southey	Davidson	Shellbrook
Dalmeny	Langenburg	St. Walburg	Esterhazy	Spiritwood
Debden	Lanigan	Strasbourg	Fort Qu'Appelle	Wadena
Eastend	Luseland	Turtleford	Hudson Bay	Watrous
Elrose	Macklin	Vonda	Indian Head	Wynyard
Eston	Midale	Wakaw	Kamsack	
Fillmore	Naicam	Watson	Kipling	
Foam Lake	Neilburg	Wawota		
Gravelbourg	Nokomis	Whitewood		
Grenfell	Ponteix	Wilkie		
Gull Lake	Porcupine Plain	Wolseley		
Herbert	Preeceville			

The group of 22 includes all but one (Foam Lake) of the 15 communities that were reclassified from PSC status between 1995 and 2001. Six of the remaining eight were reclassified from PSC to FCC between 1990 and 1995 while one (Leader) was reclassified between 1981 and 1990. The final FCC in this group, Lumsden, has retained this status since 1961.

A comparison of the profiles of the two subgroups in Table 13 indicates that, while the two groups are generally similar, the larger group of 22 has a greater complement of consumer functions present at that level and frequently has multiple outlets of these functions. For the group of 50 smaller places, fewer functions are routinely present and multiple outlets are less common. Manufacturing firms are much more likely to be present in the group of 22 than in the 50 smaller places. Both subgroups have selective complements of producer services with the 22 larger places having an average 50 percent more outlets than the smaller centres. Schools and special care centres are common to both subgroups.

Average population size in the group of 22 is almost twice that of the group of 50, although there is considerable variation within each subgroup. Consequently the total populations of the two subgroups are roughly similar: 36,684 for the 22 larger communities, 41,273 for the group of 50 smaller FCCs. In total, the population residing in the 72 FCCs equals 77,957, a little under 8 percent of the population of Saskatchewan. Table 14 contains a list of the 72 places with their subgroup designation.

CHAPTER 6

Economic Development and the Mining and Manufacturing Industries

Economic development is a term, often used with additional adjectives—regional, urban, rural—when discussing ways in which employment and income might be increased in some area of the province. In everyday conversation, a single project such as a new factory, a new electrical generating facility or a new intensive livestock operation is often referred to as development.

Strictly speaking, however, economic development—regional, urban, or rural—refers to an ongoing process. The new factory, or any other new activity, may contribute to the development process, but individual investments do not by themselves constitute economic development. In addition, most individual investments are too small to initiate a process which is continuous. Any new investment, in a factory or any other activity, will nevertheless have an impact on the local economy in which it is situated.

Analyses of the impact of an investment may conveniently be divided into the construction phase and the operational phase. The construction phase is typically short and intensive as the facilities which will be used in the operational phase are created. The number of employees during the construction phase will often exceed the number required in the operational phase.

Again, in everyday conversation, an appraisal of an investment often considers only the amount of employment directly created in the operational phase although employment in the construction phase is sometimes noted as well.

A more formal appraisal would also calculate the increase in the demand for inputs required by the new investment during both construction and operation, as well as any opportunities for further use of the outputs. In a formal appraisal, this extension of the impact analysis is often done in a regional or provincial context but seldom in a local impact analysis—urban or rural—because local industrial linkages are usually very limited.

There is an additional important impact, however, which is almost always overlooked even in formal rural and urban impact assessments. This is consideration of the local final demand linkages. As will become apparent in the following section, the impact varies considerably from one location to the next in rural space and among communities of different functional levels.

The Local Multiplier

The multiplier refers to the change in the total income which results from an increase in some autonomous expenditure.[4] The portion of the initial increase in autonomous expenditure which is paid to local factor (land, labour, capital) owners, leads to an even greater expansion of local income as the initial income is spent and respent. The process comes to an end when "leakages" from the spending stream, in the form of savings, taxes and imports, reduce to zero the increments in the flow of spending and respending. While saving rates and taxes will not vary much from place to place within a province, the same cannot be said of imports which, in this context, would include any purchases by local businesses or consumers from a wholesaler or other seller located elsewhere in the province or beyond.

Community-level multipliers for Saskatchewan were estimated in two studies (Olfert and Stabler 1994; Olfert and Stabler 1999). In the first of these studies, community level multipliers were estimated for each of the six functional levels in the trade centre hierarchy. These own-community multipliers identified the total local increase in expenditures, at each hierarchical level, occasioned by an autonomous increase in demand at that specific level.

The multiplier analysis was extended in the second study by estimating *cross-community*, *system-wide* (trade centre), and *level-specific* multipliers. Cross-community refers to the impact on community B as the result of an autonomous expenditure increase initiated in community A; system-wide refers to the sum of the own-community plus all cross-community induced effects. The level-specific multiplier is the sum of the own-community multiplier at a given level plus the cross-community impact at that level resulting from out-shopping from lower levels.

Table 15
Own- and Cross-Community, System-Wide, and Level-Specific Impact Multipliers
in the Trade Centre Hierarchy

Spending Origin	MCC	FCC	PSC	CSC	SWR	PWR	System-wide (row total)
MCC	1.0951	0.0242	0.0551	0.0335	0.1027	0.1328	1.4434
FCC		1.1762	0.0242	0.0262	0.0794	0.1374	1.4434
PSC			1.2502	0.0191	0.0584	0.1157	1.4434
CSC				1.3349	0.0122	0.0964	1.4434
SWR					1.3818	0.0616	1.4434
PWR						1.4434	1.4434
Level-specific (col. total)	1.0951	1.2004	1.3295	1.4137	1.6345	1.9873	

Table 15 identifies the multipliers just discussed. The entries on the diagonal in Table 15—1.0951, 1.1762, etc.—are the own-community multipliers. For example, each $100 of new autonomous expenditure (in value-added terms) at the FCC level, will lead to a total increase in income at the FCC level of $117.62—the initial $100 plus $17.62 of induced spending. The multipliers are larger at successively higher levels in the trade centre system because the leakages in the form of imports diminish.

---

4. Autonomous expenditures are those which are considered to be independent of the level of current income. Thus, from a pre-project perspective, local investment expenditures made during the construction phase as well as locally earned wages, rents, interest, and profits paid during both construction and operation would be considered autonomous. Wages, rents, interest, and profits are referred to as factor payments. The sum of these payments is also referred to as value-added.

Table 16
Distribution of Induced Effects (Urban=SWR+PWR) of an Autonomous Expenditure Increase

Expenditure Originating at:	Rural Impact	Urban Impact	% of Impact in Rural
MCC	0.2079	0.2355	46.88
FCC	0.2266	0.2168	51.11
PSC	0.2693	0.1741	60.73
CSC	0.3348	0.1086	75.51

The cross-community multiplier effects are shown as the off-diagonal entries such as .0242, .0551, etc. in the case of MCCs. These are interpreted as follows: for each $100 new autonomous (value-added) expenditure at the MCC level there will be an induced increase in spending of $2.42 at the FCC level, $5.51 at PSC, $3.35 at CSC, $10.27 at SWR, and $13.28 at the PWR level.

The row totals represent the system-wide multipliers and are identical (1.4434) regardless of where in the trade centre hierarchy the expenditure originates, i.e., the distribution of the impacts (over trade centre levels) differs depending on the origin but not the total system-wide impact.

Column totals represent, for each level, the sum of cross- plus own-community multiplier effects. For example, the $100 expenditure at each level in the system simultaneously will translate into an impact of only $109.51 at the MCC level but will rise to $198.73 at the PWR level. These column totals are the level-specific multipliers.

The pattern of the multiplier effects is informative of the economic development effects of new expenditures at any level. In particular it is apparent that the induced effects that follow from an autonomous (value-added) expenditure increase at the MCC or FCC levels is greater at the top of the hierarchy, in the SWR plus PWR levels, than at the level where the expenditure was actually initiated.

The pattern of small cross-community multipliers up through the CSC level also confirms the habit of rural dwellers to bypass intermediate-level centres as the population in and surrounding lower level centres travels to communities at the top of the hierarchy to shop for items not available, or not purchased, in their home community.

The striking conclusion of these observations is that a new factory or intensive livestock operation situated in, or near to, an MCC level community will actually produce a greater induced final demand impact in the SWR and PWR cities than in rural Saskatchewan.

The distribution of induced impacts between urban (defined in this instance as SWR and PWR centres) and rural Saskatchewan (all other centres), following an autonomous (value-added) expenditure increase in one of the four lowest levels in the hierarchy is shown in Table 16. From this table it is apparent that only investments at, or near, PSC or CSC communities capture a significant majority of the induced impacts in rural Saskatchewan.

Mining and Manufacturing

Conventional wisdom is that the development of a mine or the attraction of one or more manufacturing plants will enhance a community's fortunes. Our study of Saskatchewan's trade centres over a 40-year period provides a qualified verification of this proposition. The extent to which fortunes are enhanced, however, depends not only upon the magnitude of direct employment that the new activity generates but also on the level of wages that it pays. The nature of the economic development impact is also influenced by the trade centre status of the recipient community at the time of the autonomous investment and its proximity to higher level centres. The following review of the experience of Saskatchewan communities that have had mines or manufacturing firms locate in or near them permits observations on each of these influences.

Mining Communities

Creation of a major mine in the vicinity of a community can produce a local boom in housing and commercial development. Several dramatic examples of this phenomenon were apparent in Saskatchewan during and after the 1960s when potash mines were developed at several locations in the central and southeastern parts of the province.

In a previous study (Stabler and Olfert 1992) the impact of developing a mine in the vicinity of remote rural communities was investigated over a 30-year period (1961–90). Communities were divided into two groups: those close to mines which employed fewer than 50 workers and those employing 50 or more.

There were 11 remote rural communities adjacent to mines which employed fewer than 50 workers. The population, the number and the types of businesses present in these 11 communities were compared, over the 1961–90 period, with other remote communities initially occupying the same functional classification but with no mines in the immediate vicinity. In the case of these 11 communities, no systematic differences from the comparison group could be detected. This was not seen as a surprising result since employment at the mines was small and was drawn from a large geographic area rather than exclusively from the closest centre. We do not pursue the experience of these 11 communities further but rather conclude that employment of this limited magnitude is unlikely to have any noticeable effect on the viability of the adjacent community.

Ten additional communities were identified in the 1992 study which were close to mines employing 50 or more people. Of these 10, however, four (Allan, Colonsay, Delisle, and Vanscoy) are close enough to Saskatoon to share in the residential spillover of the larger centre. A fifth, Estevan, is itself an SWR centre and, as such, plays a major role in the provision of trade and services to a large area in southeastern Saskatchewan. While mining employment is undoubtedly beneficial to these communities, we did not think that we could separate its effect from these other influences. Thus these five communities were excluded from further consideration.

For the remaining five communities, a definite positive influence was apparent. In each case, a large amount of employment was created with the development of the mine. In the cases of Coronach, Esterhazy, Lanigan, and Rocanville, which expanded during the 1961–81 period, a substantial increase in population and the development of residential suburbs followed. Public infrastructure was added and some commercial development accompanied the population increase. Community growth, occasioned by the opening of the mines, did not generate a process of continuous expansion, however. These communities did not rise in status in the central place hierarchy, nor did they become locations which attracted any substantial amount of other rural-based activity. Rather, the pattern following an initial substantial expansion was one of gradual population loss from the peak attained, accompanied by gradual decline in trade centre status. The experience of the five communities studied is extended to the present for this study and recorded in Table 17. Mining employment of town residents (from Statistics Canada) is included in parentheses following the name of the community.[5] Total employment is greater than the numbers shown, of course, when in-

---

5. Even within this group, Coronach is somewhat of an anomaly because there are more town residents employed in power generation than in the mining operation itself.

Table 17
Experience of Five Small Communities with Substantial Mining Employment

Community (mining employment)	1961	1971	1981	1991	1996	2001
Bienfait (120)						
Population	842	844	834	847	826	–
Reference[1]	880	938	951	908	829	–
Status	PSC	–	FCC	MCC	MCC	MCC
Coronach (50)						
Population	395	374	1,010	906	949	–
Reference[2]	395	398	347	345	296	–
Status	FCC	–	FCC	FCC	MCC	FCC
Esterhazy (270)						
Population	1,114	3,087	3,219	2,993	2,601	–
Reference[3]	1,078	1,049	1,086	1,010	988	–
Status	CSC	–	CSC	PSC	PSC	FCC
Lanigan (130)						
Population	516	1,468	1,745	1,382	1,368	–
Reference[4]	517	467	563	555	515	–
Status	PSC	–	PSC	PSC	FCC	FCC
Rocanville (115)						
Population	496	869	956	849	875	–
Reference[5]	496	581	553	550	524	–
Status	PSC	–	FCC	FCC	MCC	FCC

[1] Reference Group: Big River, Ituna, Kelvington, Ponteix, Whitewood
[2] Reference Group: Elbow, Invermay, Sedley, Sheho, White Fox
[3] Reference Group: Gull Lake, Leader, Radville, Shellbrook, Wolseley
[4] Reference Group: Hafford, Leroy, Radisson, Waldheim, Yellow Grass
[5] Reference Group: Leask, Norquay, Raymore, Rockglen, Saltcoats.

commuters are taken into account. The population of each of the mining communities, recorded immediately beneath the place-name, is compared with a reference group of five communities which were of approximately the same size in 1961. The third line, Status, refers to the trade centre classification of the mining community at each date.

Bienfait represents another perspective on relative location and the influence of mining employment. Coal mining has long been an important employer in the Estevan area. At the time of our initial observation, Bienfait was classified in the Partial Shopping Centre category. Its population, 842 in 1961, has remained virtually constant at 835 in 1981 and 826 in 1996. Its functional classification declined to Full Convenience Centre in 1981 and down to Minimum Convenience Centre in 1990, however. Because of its location, only 11 kilometres from Estevan, Bienfait was unable to retain any but the very lowest-order commercial activities as shopping patterns were extended to geographically larger areas during the 1960s and 1970s.

Conclusions with Respect to Mining

In summary, mining employment provides a non-agricultural source of employment and income to rural residents living within commuting distance of the mine. Further, during the 1960s and the 1970s, the creation of large mines near smaller rural communities resulted in a doubling or even tripling of the 1961 populations of those centres accompanied by substantial expansion of the housing stock. Public infrastructure expanded and some consumer services followed. No community rose in trade centre status, however, because the mining communities could not compete for local retail dominance with larger, relatively close communities whose trading areas already encircled the mining centres. Very little additional rural-based development occurred in these communities either. It may be speculated that the above-average wages paid by the mining companies discouraged the location of activities that could otherwise pay lower wages by seeking an alternative location.

Nevertheless, Coronach, Esterhazy, Lanigan, and Rocanville are all larger now than they were in 1961 and are much larger than communities which were the same size in 1961 but have not experienced a major mining or other development in their vicinity. Further, most of the reference communities experienced greater decline in trade centre status than did the mining communities (except for Bienfait).

Within the functional categories that the mining communities are classified with in 2001, all have populations well above the respective group means.[6] Like bedroom communities, the mining centres may be thought of as special purpose communities which attained their size for reasons other than their role as trade centres.

Manufacturing Communities

Unlike mines which are relatively few in number, manufacturing firms are numerous. There are approximately 2,800 manufacturing plants in the province and, while they are present at all levels of the hierarchy, manufacturing is highly concentrated at the top of the system. The 18 communities in the top three trade centre classifications account for 85 percent of Saskatchewan's manufacturing plants.

The 580 communities in the three lower classifications share 400 manufacturing plants. Each PSC has three or more, while about 90 percent of the FCCs have one or more. At the MCC level, fewer than one in five centres have a manufacturing plant.

Manufacturing employment at the MCC, FCC, and PSC levels is limited even in those communities which do have one or more plants. When bedroom and mining communities are removed from this set, very few communities remain which have 50 or more employees.

In order to assess the importance of the presence of a manufacturing plant on a community's overall economic performance, an approach similar to that used to investigate the contributions of a mine was adopted. Communities in the MCC, FCC, and PSC classifications with 50 or more manufacturing employees were identified and their performance compared, over a 40 year period, with other communities of initially the same size but with little or no manufacturing employment. The results of these comparisons are reported in Table 18.

At the MCC level, most communities with 50 or more workers employed in manufacturing are in the immediate vicinity of Saskatoon.[7] Manufacturers may have chosen these locations in part because they are near a major city with all the implied amenities and services. Also, these places are close enough to serve as bedroom communities for Saskatoon.

One remote MCC community that does have substantial manufacturing employment is St. Brieux with nearly 200 employees. We use St. Brieux as the only manufacturing MCC for comparison purposes.[8]

---

6. Esterhazy is classified with the top 22 FCCs in 2001 (discussed in Chapter 5). Lanigan, Coronach, and Rocanville are grouped with the 50 smaller FCCs. Bienfait is grouped with the 72 largest MCCs. Except for Bienfait, the commercial and infrastructure profiles of the mining communities are similar to those for the group in which they are included.

7. Delisle, Langham, Martensville, Osler, Waldheim and Warman fall into this category.

8. Annaheim would have been another MCC candidate but this community was one of those omitted in the original 1961study. Thus information for Annaheim for the historical period was not available.

Chapter 6: Economic Development and the Mining and Manufacturing Industries

Table 18
Experience of MCC, FCC, and PSC Communities with Substantial Manufacturing Employment
1961–2001

Community	1961	1971	1981	1991	1996	2001
MCC Level						
St. Brieux–Population	364	378	393	437	507	–
Reference[1]	364	382	319	276	250	–
Status	FCC	–	MCC	MCC	FCC	MCC
FCC Level[2]						
Big River–Population	896	889	947	839	826	–
Reference[3]	899	1,001	1,048	1,034	931	–
Status	FCC	FCC	FCC	PSC	PSC	FCC
Watson–Population	910	818	929	872	837	–
Reference[4]	910	978	1,083	1,040	946	–
Status	PSC	–	PSC	PSC	FCC	FCC
Biggar–Population	2,702	2,644	2,660	2,332	2,351	–
Reference[5]	2,620	2,657	3,126	3,126	3,023	–
Status	CSC	–	CSC	PSC	PSC	FCC
Carrot River–Population	930	950	1,205	1,046	1,032	–
Reference[6]	928	1,149	1,322	1,271	1,185	–
Status	PSC	–	PSC	FCC	FCC	FCC
Wynyard–Population	1,956	1,930	2,286	2,092	1,954	–
Reference[7]	1,993	2,190	2,323	2,154	2,025	–
Status	CSC	–	CSC	PSC	PSC	FCC
Hudson Bay–Population	1,601	2,083	2,575	2,065	1,883	–
Reference[8]	1,558	1,478	1,655	1,570	1,510	–
Status	PSC	–	CSC	PSC	PSC	FCC
PSC Level						
Moosomin–Population	1,781	2,447	2,576	2,510	2,420	–
Reference[9]	1,772	1,383	2,000	1,891	1,816	–
Status	CSC	–	CSC	PSC	PSC	PSC

[1] Reference Group: Dodsland, Holdfast, Manor, Rhein
[2] FCC communities are arranged in ascending order of manufacturing employment
[3] Reference Group: Kelvington, Ponteix, Preeceville, Whitewood
[4] Reference Group: Davidson, Ponteix, Preeceville, Whitewood
[5] Reference Group: Assiniboia, Kamsack, Kindersley, Rosetown
[6] Reference Group: Davidson, Foam Lake, Preeceville
[7] Reference Group: Canora, Indian Head, Shaunavon, Unity
[8] Reference Group: Eston, Fort Qu'Appelle, Gravelbourg, Watrous, Wilkie
[9] Reference Group: Unity, Wilkie, Indian Head.

At the FCC level, there are six remote communities with over 50 people employed in manufacturing: Big River, Biggar, and Watson have between 50 and 100, Carrot River just over 100, while Hudson Bay and Wynyard have over 200 employees.

At the PSC level, Moosomin is the only community with over 50 manufacturing jobs.

The statistics in Table 18 do not provide an unequivocal statement. When the population growth of the eight manufacturing communities combined is compared with that of the 19 combined reference communities, the results are virtually identical. The manufacturing communities, as a group, gained 6 percent in population between 1961 and 1996. The 19 communities which had nearly identical populations as the manufacturing communities in 1961, gained 5.2 percent.

At the MCC and PSC levels, St. Brieux and Moosomin outperformed the reference communities. But at the FCC level, where the largest manufacturing jobs are recorded, the combined reference communities gained 6.9 percent in population while the manufacturing communities (combined) lost 1.3 percent. Further, all but one of the manufacturing centres (Big River) had declined in trade centre status between 1961 and 2001. Five were one classification lower in 2001 and two had dropped two categories.

Turning now to Complete Shopping Centres, of the eight communities at this level

Table 19
Comparison of Communities with Complete Shopping Centre Classification in 2001
with 21 Other Centres Classified CSC in 1961

Communities	1961	1971	1981	1990	1995	1996
8 CSCs in 2001 Population	3,323	3,789	4,450	4,500	4,568	4,364
21 CSCs in 1961[1] Population	1,769	1,924	2,055	1,937	1,890	1,848

[1] The 21 communities are: Biggar, Canora, Esterhazy, Eston, Fort Qu'Appelle, Gravelbourg, Gull Lake, Indian Head, Kamsack, Kerrobert, Leader, Maple Creek, Moosomin, Outlook, Rosetown, Shaunavon, Unity, Wadena, Watrous, Wilkie, Wynyard. The 1995 and 1996 populations are not strictly comparable since 1995 (and earlier years) is Saskatchewan Health population and 1996 is Statistics Canada Census population.

in 2001, five had over 100 manufacturing jobs. All five of these communities had retained their CSC status between 1961 and 2001. The only other community retaining CSC status throughout this 40-year period was Kindersley with approximately 75 manufacturing jobs. Two other centres classified as CSC in 2001 (Assiniboia and Melville) had been classified as CSC in 1961 but had dropped to PSC in the interim only to subsequently regain their CSC status. These centres had the smallest number of manufacturing jobs of the CSC centres in 2001.

In 1961 there were 21 other communities in the CSC category. Only one of these (Wynyard) had over 100 manufacturing jobs in 2001. The other 20 had fewer than 100 manufacturing jobs and all had declined one or two tiers in trade centre classification. In Table 19 the eight communities classified as CSC in 2001 are compared with the other 21 places similarly classified in 1961. Clearly the eight thoroughly outperformed the other 21.

Conclusions with Respect to Manufacturing

In deriving some tentative conclusions regarding the effect of manufacturing activity, it is necessary to keep several considerations in mind. Entrepreneurs often exercise some care in selecting a community in which to situate their plant. Thus a chicken and egg question arises. Were the communities that retained CSC status throughout already sufficiently attractive because of their size and location on the transportation network, or did the local commercial outlets have a sufficiently good reputation that they were emerging as locally dominant communities which then drew the manufacturing firms to their already viable locations? Or was it the growth of the manufacturing activity which added population and strengthened the other commercial sectors? It is not possible to know with certainty.

Giving the benefit of the doubt, perhaps it can be concluded from this that 100 or more manufacturing jobs can contribute to the *economic development* of a community which is well situated on the regional transportation network and which has a sufficient complement of trade and service outlets for it to play a dominant role in the regional trade centre system. In such communities the multiplier effect will induce some further expansion in final-demand-linked activities.

The experience of St. Brieux, on the other hand, which is poorly situated and whose trade centre status had declined before the manufacturing presence expanded to its present size, illustrates that even a relatively large manufacturing presence is unlikely to reverse past decline in trade centre status though it may stabilize or even generate a moderate increase in population.

The number of communities compared in Tables 18 and 19 is obviously too small to permit strong conclusions but, to the extent that it is possible to derive a message from these data, it might be as follows: substantial manufacturing employment can contribute to the stability and perhaps even enhance the trade centre status of a community that is favourably situated and presently viable within the trade centre network.

A majority of the induced effects of development following investment in larger, already viable, rural trade centres will be realized in rural areas. Such investment will make additional, subsequent investments more likely. It will contribute to the development process.

For communities that are poorly situated or have already declined to Full or Minimum Convenience status, even substantial manufacturing employment may lead only to results similar to those observed in the section on mining. That is, even substantial employment may do no more than stabilize the population. It is unlikely to reverse or even sustain the trade centre role once it has fallen below a critical level. Further, because leakages are so high from such communities, the major portion of the induced development following the investment is transferred to the province's major centres.

CHAPTER 7

Infrastructure and Other Considerations

In this chapter our focus is on identifying those communities which have the capacity to support significant regional or rural development. For this inquiry we focus on the 24 communities in the top four functional categories of the trade centre hierarchy plus the largest 22 Full Convenience Centres identified in the separate cluster analysis of this functional category. A map showing these centres is provided in Figure 2. Our focus is on communities because for many years major cities and larger towns have been the engines for job creation, not only in Saskatchewan but throughout the developed world. This is not to deny that resource-based development has been a locally important source of job creation. Indeed, this will likely continue to be the case. Compared with urban-based activities, however, especially the service industries, rural resource-based employment continues to decline in importance.

Our analysis to this point consisted of evaluations of Saskatchewan's communities, using a variety of techniques. The cluster analysis was used to produce subsets of similar centres. The discriminant analysis was used to verify the groups produced with the cluster analysis. The multiplier analysis identified the amount of induced income generation that would follow from an autonomous investment at each level in the hierarchy as well as the amount of additional induced income generated in rural space as a consequence.

In chapter 6 our investigation focussed on whether significant mining or manufacturing employment could alter the path a community was following as part of the ongoing reorganization of the trade centre hierarchy.

Each evaluation reinforced the others. Each emphasized, in a different but complementary way, a well-defined hierarchical structure in which the strength and diversity of individual centres, in terms of consumer and producer services as well as infrastructure, reflects the size of the consumer and business markets they serve.

The location pattern of producers, especially agriculture and other resource-based industries, does not follow a hierarchical pattern because resources are distributed according to natural criteria. The distribution of manufacturers, however, does adhere (with a few notable exceptions) to the hierarchical pattern because the concentration of population in larger towns and cities assures the presence of a labour pool and a variety of skills. In addition, transportation hubs are associated with larger urban places, business services are concentrated at the top of the hierarchy, and adequate housing and infrastructure is typically available.

But even when there is a significant departure from the hierarchical pattern, in the location of a major mine or manufacturer, this neither destroys nor modifies the

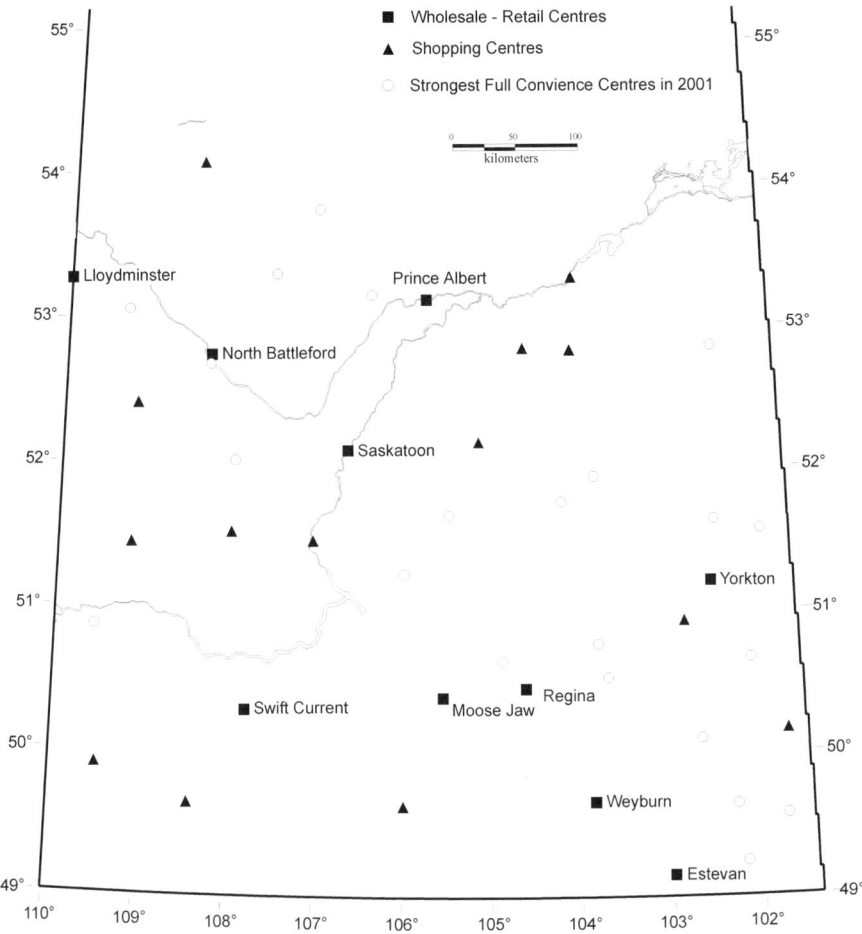

Figure 2. Top 46 Communities in Saskatchewan, 2001

ongoing pattern of change within the trade centre system, although it may increase and/or stabilize the individual community's population. No example exists, in Saskatchewan, of such investment initiating a process of sustained development in a small community nor of increasing the community's trade centre status.

With this summary as background, we now turn to a discussion of the capacity of Saskatchewan's communities for significant future regional or rural development.

Commuting Patterns

One indicator of a community's potential for hosting future development is indicated by the extent to which it currently provides employment for members of the labour force residing in its vicinity. To this end, data on the number of people commuting to work in each of the 24 centres in the top four functional categories, as well as to the largest 22 Full Convenience Centres, was collected. These data are arrayed in Tables 20 and 21. Also shown is the number of workers commuting out from these centres to work elsewhere. These data were constructed from special tabulations obtained from Statistics Canada and refer to the 1996 commuting flows.

Chapter 7: Infrastructure and Other Considerations

Table 20
Commuters to and from Saskatchewan's 46 Major Communities, 1996

Community	Commuters[1] In	Commuters[1] Out	Community	Commuters[1] In	Commuters[1] Out
PWR			**FCC**		
Regina	9,220	5,740	Battleford	135	1,255
Saskatoon	12,015	7,075	Big River	445	60
SWR			Biggar	345	80
Estevan	1,530	520	Canora	355	110
Lloydminster	2,115	2,210	Carlyle	430	80
Moose Jaw	1,905	2,675	Davidson	345	40
North Battleford	2,595	955	Esterhazy	1,060	155
Prince Albert	4,085	2,330	Ft. Qu'Appelle	870	130
Swift Current	1,870	640	Hudson Bay	775	85
Weyburn	1,050	420	Indian Head	320	155
Yorkton	2,445	585	Kamsack	415	30
CSC			Kipling	275	20
Assiniboia	515	40	Leader	na	na
Humboldt	895	350	Lumsden	na	na
Kindersley	580	130	Maidstone	290	45
Meadow Lake	1,035	365	Oxbow	215	110
Melfort	905	455	Redvers	280	20
Melville	945	160	Shellbrook	420	85
Nipawin	835	195	Spiritwood	320	40
Tisdale	835	165	Wadena	350	75
PSC			Watrous	380	95
Maple Creek	365	105	Wynyard	635	75
Moosomin	515	80			
Outlook	420	95			
Rosetown	560	105			
Shaunavon	300	50			
Unity	475	140			

[1]All numbers end in 5 or 0 because of a "random rounding" procedure used by Statistics Canada.
Source: Statistics Canada. Special Tabulations, 1996 Census.

In Table 20 the number of in- and out-commuters are shown by individual centre. In Table 21 selected statistics are shown by hierarchy level. These data provide a number of interesting observations. The aggregate statistics in Table 21 reflect a pattern consistent with the other measures of hierarchical strength. Commuting into and out of the 18 centres in the top three functional categories accounts for 80 and 88 percent, respectively, of all commutes into and out of the 46 centres under consideration. These numbers reflect the extent to which jobs, and thus the labour force, are

Table 21
Commuting Statistics by Hierarchy Level in Saskatchewan, 1996

Hierarchy Level	Commuters Total In	Commuters Total Out	Commuters Average In	Commuters Average Out	Commuters % of Total In	Commuters % of Total Out	Commuters Cum. % In	Commuters Cum. % Out
PWR	21,235	12,815	10,618	6,408	37.5	45.2	37.5	45.2
SWR	17,595	10,335	2,199	1,292	31.0	36.5	68.5	81.7
CSC	6,545	1,860	818	232	11.5	6.6	80.0	88.3
PSC	2,635	572	439	95	4.6	2.0	84.6	90.3
FCC[1]	8,660	2,745	433	137	15.3	9.7	100.00	100.00
			(379)	(139)				

[1]The statistics at the FCC level exclude Leader and Lumsden. The numbers in parentheses are the level averages after resource communities are excluded.

concentrated in a small number of places in Saskatchewan. The other 26[9] PSCs and FCCs account for 20 percent of in-commuters and 12 percent of out-commuters. In-commutes to these 46 centres accounted for 92 percent of all Saskatchewan urban-destined commutes in 1996. Total in- and out-commutes to these centres account for 84 percent of all commutes to work in 1996.

At the individual community level, the statistics reflect the aggregate pattern but, in addition, provide detail specific to the centre itself. It can be noted from the two tables, for example, that the proportion of out-commuters is even more highly concentrated at the PWR and SWR levels than is the proportion of in-commuters. For Saskatoon and Regina, especially, but for some of the SWR centres as well, the out-commuters are people who have chosen to live in a major urban area and commute to jobs outside the city. School teachers, nurses, administrators, sales representatives, potash and even uranium miners—people who, in an earlier time, would have lived in or nearer to the places where they worked—are all represented. The location of businesses and public infrastructure, and thus the concentration of commuters, in the largest places reflects the access to provincial, national, and international markets afforded by the largest centres.

Other particular circumstances are reflected in the commuting data. Movement from one side of the city to the other explains the relatively large in- and out-numbers for Lloydminster and the large number of out-commuters from Battleford to North Battleford. Commuting to work at an activity immediately adjacent to, but outside of, the city is indicated by the high out-commuting figures for Moose Jaw (Canadian Forces Base) and Prince Albert (forest products plants). Communities with large resource extractive or processing industries (Meadow Lake, Esterhazy, Hudson Bay) stand out as well with in-commuting numbers substantially in excess of the average for communities at their level. In fact, if Esterhazy and Hudson Bay are removed from the FCC group, the average in-commuting for the remaining 18 FCCs in Table 20 is 379 rather than the 433 when they are included. These numbers are shown in parentheses in Table 21. Finally, in the case of Fort Qu'Appelle, the large number of in-commuters is explained by the dispersed settlement pattern around the lakes in the Qu'Appelle valley close to Fort Qu'Appelle.

Review of Research on Infrastructure

In recent years there has been a notable amount of research focussed on the relationship between investment in infrastructure and either economic growth generally or productivity growth in specific sectors. The results of this research are not unequivocal but, on balance, seem to suggest, at the state or provincial level, that investment in public infrastructure (highways, water, sewer, telecommunications) does increase the productivity of certain types of industries (manufacturing is a typical focus of attention). This may be particularly true if the state or province lags the nation and is playing catch up, provided that it does not start too far back in the race and is otherwise well endowed with labour and resources (Morrison and Schwartz 1996). It may also be particularly true if the investment is made in highly productive regions rather than depressed regions (Yamano and Ohkawara 2000). When the social costs of the investment (leaving the money in the hands of the taxpayers or using it for an alternative investment) are taken into account, net benefits may or may not be positive (which emphasizes the need for selectivity in making the investments).

Many studies have been conducted on the regional impact of the interstate highway system in the United States, and as with all such inquiries, these results are not

---

9. Commuting data were not available for Leader and Lumsden.

Chapter 7: Infrastructure and Other Considerations

unambiguous. In a recent study, Chandra and Thompson (2000) summarize numerous preceding studies and extend the empirical analysis on this topic. The conclusion seems to be, first, that significant highway improvement has a differential impact across industries: certain industries (manufacturing) grow as a result of reduced transportation costs, but for others the impact is ambiguous. Second, highway improvement affects the spatial allocation of economic activity within regions: interstate highways raise the level of economic activity in counties through which they pass directly, but draw activity away from adjacent counties, thereby leaving the net level of economic activity more or less unchanged in non-metropolitan (rural) areas. If the non-metropolitan county has a "small" town (25,000 population in the United States), it is likely the beneficiary of this consolidation and relocation. The rapid consolidation of Saskatchewan's trade and service activities into fewer, larger rural communities, which coincided with the extension of the paved highway network beginning in the late 1950s, is consistent with the experience reported by Chandra and Thompson.

Several years ago, there was much speculation that the "communications revolution"—small powerful computers, the internet, reduced long distance telephone rates and so on—would make substantial decentralization of the labour force possible. Thus, it was argued that rural areas might well benefit from the new technology and experience a revival. History has provided only limited support for these presumptions. In a few places, routine data processing and/or telemarketing firms have located in small rural communities. At the other end of the skills spectrum, a few very talented "lone eagles" and "telecommuters" are able to work from their location of choice but most pick high-amenity locations. For the most part, however, the technical opportunities made possible by greatly improved communications technologies have benefited primarily existing business firms in small towns and rural areas, increasing their efficiency, rather than leading to an influx of people or new businesses (Economic Research Service 1998).

The conclusion to this section seems to be that adequate infrastructure is required for development but that investment in infrastructure does not make development inevitable. If other provinces and states are investing regularly in infrastructure, then a certain amount of investment in Saskatchewan is necessary just to stay in the race. Perhaps a state or province can only gain on its competitor jurisdictions by being first and by systematically investing more. Within the province, however, selective investment in infrastructure enhances some areas relative to others and results in an internal spatial reorganization.

Infrastructure in Saskatchewan
Highways

Saskatchewan is served by an extensive network of paved highways and gravel roads. Paved highways are divided into three major categories which reflect their strength and durability. Weight limits have been established for each type of highway. The maximum allowable weights are permitted on *primary* highways 12 months per year. Highways 1, 16, and 2 are examples of primary highways. A second set of highways allows primary weights for 10 months of the year and are referred to as *winter primary* highways. During May and June the weight limits on winter primary highways drop down to the weight limits for *secondary* highways, the lowest of the three (paved) categories. Highways 204 (North Battleford to Meadow Lake) and 13 (Weyburn to Carlyle) are examples of winter primary highways. The secondary system is the most extensive and is found throughout the province. Highway 21 from the United States border, through Maple Creek, Kindersley and Unity to Pierceland is an example of a secondary highway.

As a generalization, weight limits are 10–20 percent lower on secondary than on

Table 22
Highway Access for 46 Saskatchewan Communities by Highway-Type Connections

Community	No. of Connections			Community	No. of Connections		
	Pri.	W. Pri.	Sec.		Pri.	W. Pri.	Sec.
PWR				FCC			
Regina	4			Battleford	3	1	
Saskatoon	4			Big River		2	1
SWR				Biggar	2	2	
Estevan	3		1	Canora	3	1	
Lloydminster	4			Carlyle	2	2	
Moose Jaw	4			Davidson	2		1
N. Battleford	3	1		Esterhazy	2		1
Prince Albert	3	1		Ft. Qu'Appelle	2		2
Swift Current	3		1	Hudson Bay		2	2
Weyburn	2	1	1	Indian Head	2		1
Yorkton	4			Kamsack	1	1	2
CSC				Kipling			2
Assiniboia	1		3	Leader			3
Humboldt	2		2	Lumsden	2		1
Kindersley	2		2	Maidstone	2		2
Meadow Lake	2		2	Oxbow	4		
Melfort	3		1	Redvers		2	2
Melville	2		2	Shellbrook	1	2	
Nipawin	1	2	1	Spiritwood			4
Tisdale	2	2		Wadena	2	2	
PSC				Watrous	2		
Maple Creek	2		2	Wynyard	2		
Moosomin	3		1				
Outlook		2	2				
Rosetown	3	1					
Shaunavon	1		3				
Unity	2		2				

primary highways. Thus the cost of transportation could be substantially higher for a firm which was served only by secondary highways, if the firm had a large volume of heavy in or out traffic.

Of the 46 communities under discussion, 39 are connected by at least one primary highway. For four communities, the highest quality connections are winter primary highways; only three communities are connected solely by secondary highways.

In Table 22, the types of highways connecting each community are identified. The coding system refers to the number of *directions* from the community and the *type of highway* leading in each of the four possible directions. The maximum attainable score for any community for any highway type is four regardless of the actual number of connections. Thus from Regina or Saskatoon primary highways lead N-S-E-W and they are coded with 4s in the Primary Highways column. From Swift Current primary highways lead in three directions and a secondary highway in one. Leader is connected only by secondary highways which lead in three directions, etc.

In a rough way, quality of access exhibits a hierarchical pattern. Below the 10 Wholesale-Retail centres, only one community is connected by primary highways leading in four directions. Below the SWR centres only five of the remaining 36 communities are connected by primary highways leading in three directions; only two FCCs are so connected. Down through the PSC level all communities have paved highways of one type or the other leading in four directions. Of the 22 FCCs, 10 do not have four-way paved highway connections.

Chapter 7: Infrastructure and Other Considerations

Telecommunications

As with highways, Saskatchewan is served by a vast network of communications facilities. Telephone, internet, cellular, and a variety of data transmission services are available in all PWR and SWR centres as well as in most of the other 36 communities under discussion. Within some of these services there is provision for enhanced speed and volume which can be tailored to the customers' needs. Facilities and services provided by SaskTel in CSC and lower level communities are identified in Table 23. A few services are not available in some of the FCC centres.

In addition to SaskTel's offerings, Shaw Cable provides cable internet services to Saskatoon, Prince Albert, Moose Jaw, Lloydminster, Swift Current, Assiniboia, Central Butte, and Rockglen. Access Telecommunications, out of Regina, provides a similar service to Regina, Yorkton, Estevan, and Weyburn. Battleford Cable provides cable internet services to Battleford and North Battleford (discussion with company

Table 23
Telecommunications Services for 46 Saskatchewan Communities by Service Type

Selected Rural Communities	Data and Integrated Services		Internet	
	Frame Relay services	LANspan IP	High Speed	Dial Sympatico
Assiniboia		X	X	X
Battleford	X	X	X	X
Big River	X			X
Biggar	X	X	X	X
Canora	X	X	X	X
Carlyle	X		X	X
Davidson	X	X	X	X
Esterhazy	X	X	X	X
Fort Qu'Apple	X	X	X	X
Hudson Bay	X	X	X	X
Humboldt	X	X	X	X
Indian Head	X	X	X	X
Kamsack	X	X	X	X
Kindersley	X	X	X	X
Kipling	X	X		X
Maple Creek	X	X	X	X
Meadow Lake	X	X	X	X
Melfort	X	X	X	X
Melville	X	X	X	X
Moosomin	X	X	X	X
Leader	X			X
Lumsden	X	X	X	X
Maidstone	X			X
Nipawin	X	X	X	X
Outlook	X	X	X	X
Oxbow	X	X	X	X
Redvers	X			X
Rosetown	X	X	X	X
Shaunavon	X	X	X	X
Shellbrook	X			X
Spiritwood	X			X
Tisdale	X	X	X	X
Unity	X	X	X	X
Wadena	X			X
Watrous	X	X	X	X
Wynyard	X	X	X	X

Source: SaskTel personal communications. January 2002.

representatives December 2001, January 2002). Thus a wider range of options is available in the Primary and Secondary Wholesale-Retail centres than at lower levels in the hierarchy.

Nevertheless, a wide variety of telecommunications services are available to the communities below the Wholesale-Retail levels. Unless a business needs to continuously transmit and receive very large volumes of data at high speeds, the existing facilities should provide an adequate service.

Telecommunications technology has advanced rapidly in the recent past. Adoption and installment of the latest technologies could produce further improvement in rural areas, not only in Saskatchewan but across much of rural North America. What the benchmark services to rural communities will eventually be remains to be defined.

Electricity and Natural Gas

A concerted effort was made to provide electricity and natural gas to rural Saskatchewan several decades ago. As a consequence, electricity and natural gas is widely available throughout most of the province's rural space. Basic electrical transmission lines and natural gas pipelines connect all of the 46 communities under consideration.

Industrial requirements for electricity and natural gas vary by activity. A few activities are intensive users of energy, many others have lower but substantial energy requirements, while the requirements for a small retail outlet will not differ much from a residential user's requirements.

An activity such as the IPSCO steel plant, or a major oil refinery, would require an unusually large amount of electricity. A major hospital or a medium-size shopping mall would require an intermediate level. Small individual retail outlets are numerous but have modest needs.

Natural gas users would have a similar pattern. There are a few very large users, such as the Kalium potash mine, a larger number of intermediate users such as a commercial grain dryer, a medium-size shopping mall, a very large hotel. Again, a large number of small users might have requirements similar to those of a residential user.

A demand for energy or power similar to that of the largest users would require some investment at any location to make it possible. Demands of the intermediate and small variety could likely be met without difficulty in any of the 46 locations (discussions with SaskEnergy and SaskPower, January 2002).

Water

Water use in communities is for municipal and industrial purposes. Requirements by industrial users vary with the type of activity. Some food-processing activities, for example, require large volumes of water equivalent in quality to that needed for drinking. Others may require large quantities but may not require it to be treated. Water use by a small retail firm may be similar to that of a residential user.

We were not able to systematically identify the availability of water for industrial purposes for the 46 communities under discussion in this chapter. Although most communities provided brochures describing their populations, businesses and infrastructure, the information provided concerning water usually described the existing system but did not indicate capacity for expansion.

With respect to municipal water supply, a technical assessment conducted in 2001 provides some information on communities grouped by population size (Sask Water Corporation 2001). Data in Table 24 describe sources of supply and average peak day water demand for 513 Saskatchewan communities. All of the communities under consideration in this chapter are included in groups five and six in Table 24.

Chapter 7: Infrastructure and Other Considerations

Table 24
Water Sources and Peak Day Flow for 513 Saskatchewan Communities, 2001

Group	1	2	3	4	5	6	All
Peak Day Demand	0 to 1.0	1.0 to 2.5	2.5 to 6.0	6.0 to 15.0	15.0 to 100.0	Over 100.0	N/A
No. of Communities	129	118	107	105	44	10	513
No. of Groundwater Communities	90	93	82	82	26	1	374
No. of Surface Water Communities	39	25	25	23	18	9	139
Approximate Population Range	1 to 100	201 to 500	201 to 500	501 to 1,000	1,001 to 10,000	over 10,000	N/A
Total 1996 Population	6,387	12,421	30,808	70,619	93,860	525, 320	739,415

Source: Sask Water Corporation, 2001.

Table 25
Infrastructure Requirements to Meet Water Quality Standards, Saskatchewan Communities, 2001

Group	1	2	3	4	5
Population Range	1 to 100	101 to 200	201 to 500	501 to 1,000	1,001 to 10,000
Total No. of Communities	129	118	107	105	44
No. of Sample Communities	13	14	15	12	10
% Requiring Upgrade to Raw Supply System	50	69	63	60	50
% Requiring Upgrade to Water Treatment Facility	92	100	81	100	88
% Requiring Upgrade to Treated Water Storage	25	62	56	47	75
% Requiring Upgrade to Water Distribution	83	77	31	20	50

Source: Sask Water Corporation, 2001.

A sample of 64 communities was selected from groups one through five for assessment of infrastructure and quality management. The 10 largest cities were requested to provide information, by mail survey, on upgrades required to meet health-related water quality objectives. The data in Table 25 are inferences by Sask Water, based on the 64 communities sampled, of upgrades required for each group. Apparently most communities in each group require upgrades to meet health-related standards for municipal water quality. One-half of the SWR Centres also indicated a need to upgrade their infrastructure. The two PWR centres and four of the SWRs did not identify any new infrastructure requirements to meet health standards.

Sewage and Solid Waste Disposal

Saskatchewan Environment and Resource Management (SERM) reports on community compliance with sewage regulations and solid waste disposal guidelines.

As with water, however, the reports identify what facilities are available and what practices are being followed. For sewage systems, there are no measures of capacity. For waste disposal, communities are asked to identify the estimated date at which

Table 26
Compliance with Solid Waste and Sewage Disposal Regulations in Saskatchewan Communities, 2001

Level of Community	Capacity[1]		Distance[2]		Designated Areas[3]						Burning[4]				Containment[5]					
					Metal		Tires		Trees		Unsorted		Approved		Compact		Cover		Fenced	
	Y	N	Y	N	Y	N	Y	N	Y	N	Y	N	Y	N	Y	N	Y	N	Y	N
PWR	2		1	1	2		1	1	1	1		2	2		2		2			2
SWR	4	1	3	2	5		4	1	4	1		5	4		4	1	4	1		5
CSC	1	1	1	1	2		1	1	2			2	2		2		2			2
PSC	6		4	2	6		6		6			6	6		5	1	5	1		6
FCC	4	5	4	5	9		6	3	9		1	8	9		6	3	6	3		9

[1] Are the grounds sufficient for more than 5 years?
[2] 500 metres from residential, commercial, industrial, institutional facilities?
[3] Designated storage areas. In addition Saskatoon, Esterhazy, and Shaunavon have storage areas for empty pesticide containers. This appears to be an RM responsibility in some places.
[4] Burning of unsorted and/or approved waste?
[5] Are compaction and/or cover guidelines complied with? Is the facility fenced?
Source: Saskatchewan Environment and Resource Management. Personal Communications. January 2002.

their disposal grounds will be filled to capacity, which is an indirect indication of their ability to process additional solid waste.

The data in Table 26 summarize the information forwarded by SERM from 24 communities which responded to our request for information. As shown in the table, most communities are in compliance with most solid waste disposal guidelines. For a few communities whose disposal grounds are nearly full, some guidelines are not being met. For these communities, expansions or new grounds are either being planned or are proposed.

With respect to sewage disposal, all but one community is in compliance with the pertinent regulations.[10] That community reports that a new sewage treatment plant will be constructed in 2004. Three additional communities providing information on solid waste disposal did not provide information on sewage disposal.

Local Economic Development Initiatives

Most rural communities with populations of 2,000, along with many smaller ones, have some type of formally organized effort to encourage economic activity. In 1993 an attempt was made to determine the types of organizations used, the techniques employed, and the extent to which efforts had been rewarded. A series of visits to 33 Prairie communities ranging from the Secondary Wholesale-Retail through to the Full Convenience level was made. The survey included 18 of those communities under discussion in this chapter. Some interviews were held with mayors and councillors, others with economic development officers and members of economic development committees. A summary of our observations from that experience is provided here since the questions of local leadership and local initiative frequently arise when discussing rural economies.

Organizations

Community economic development organizations occupy a spectrum running from loosely arranged volunteer committees to formally organized departments of local government. Most communities also either have a tourism committee or combine tourism with economic development.

The least formally organized structures consist only of an economic development committee, staffed by volunteers from the civic administration and local business and/or professional groups.

Greater formality exists when the community has employed an economic development officer, and in larger centres, there may be an economic development department with a small staff. In other instances, economic development and community planning

---

10. Sections 13(2) and 13(3) of the Water Pollution and Waterworks Regulations Act and Section 17 of the Environmental Management and Protection Act.

may be combined. Communities employing economic development officers have economic development committees, consisting either of local government employees or elected officials only, or, more commonly, of civic employees/officials and representative of business and other interest groups. In addition, a few of these committees have attempted to recruit members to represent financial, labour, rural, or farming interests. The economic development committee sets policies that the economic development officer implements. Economic development officers are typically members of these committees; if they are junior people, they may play a passive role, but if they are experienced and accomplished in the job, they may be very influential. The involvement of the mayor in any capacity seemed to be based more on personal interest than on any systematic differences in organizational structure.

In addition to their own efforts, many communities were members of larger regional organizations. Community Futures, ADD Boards, and Rural Development Corporations were common in Saskatchewan in 1993. In the meantime, Regional Economic Development Authorities have become the common provincially sponsored regional organization in Saskatchewan.

Methods of Business Development and Retention

Nearly all communities have prepared websites and brochures that describe their community's attributes: its population, labour force, major businesses, and recreational, medical, educational and social organizations. Brochures are made available to interested parties and are distributed beyond the community either through its own efforts or through those of provincial or federal government economic development agencies. Some communities have also prepared 8–15 minute video cassette tapes that describe and present visual impressions of major assets and prominent characteristics in the community. Many communities have at times taken out advertisements in national papers such as *The Globe and Mail* or even in foreign publications. Trips have also been made on occasion to Toronto or Vancouver to attempt to interest businesses in moving.

All larger communities and most of the smaller places included in the survey have either serviced, or readily serviceable, industrial land available for prospective manufacturers, wholesalers, and other potential occupants of industrial parks.

Beyond these common basic items, communities differ not only in what they do, but also in the commitment and intensity with which they pursue development objectives. Activities include a variety of approaches to recruit or initiate business, with programs designed to encourage residents to "buy local," to improve the efficiency of local business, to increase aid from senior levels of government, to promote tourism, to attract new residents, and to recruit provincial government employment or facilities.

Attempts to recruit or initiate businesses were common to all communities interviewed. In addition to the promotional efforts previously mentioned, other initiatives included using incubator malls; attempting to establish locally created equity funds (sometimes assisted by senior levels of government); facilitating the acquisition of vacant buildings for potential businesses; assisting in configuring property to meet the specific needs of a prospective client; and encouraging or assisting the business community to appoint or arrange for "mentors" who could advise the management of new or expanding businesses at critical points in the decision-making process.

Residential lots, particularly in rural centres within commuting distance of a major city, have been offered free or virtually free in some instances. Other communities have offered tax holidays to new businesses. Municipal involvement with private interests or provincial governments to develop retirement homes has also been used as a way to attract or retain population.

Effectiveness

All of the communities in the SWR and CSC categories gained enough manufacturing firms during the 1960–90 period to contribute substantially to their viability. Some of the PSCs had a similar experience, although not all did.

A number of locational preconditions appear to have been very important in influencing subsequent success. For example, below the SWR level, a number of observations were common enough across the Prairies to suggest that there were conditions that were necessary in order for manufacturing activity to develop.

Nearly all of the CSC and PSC Centres that gained an important complement of manufacturers, for example, are located in the regions of higher population density within their respective provinces. Thus eastern and southeastern portions of the settled areas of Manitoba, the northern half of the agricultural area in Saskatchewan, and the northern and corridor regions in Alberta contain virtually all of the small manufacturing communities. Further, all of these communities were locally important places in the trade centre system in the 1960s and all were conveniently located on the provincial highway network. Thus viable trade centres that were in areas of higher population density and well located with respect to highway transportation had a much better chance of gaining manufacturing firms than those missing one or more of these attributes.

The situation differed between larger and smaller communities. SWR centres, for example, all gained manufacturers regardless of the intensity of local initiative, although northern (and Alberta's corridor) communities in this classification grew faster than southern places. It seems likely that centres at this level had sufficient resident population within commuting distance to satisfy the labour force requirements of potential manufacturing firms, whereas smaller communities might not have a sufficient resident population within commuting distance. Below some threshold of population density, the likelihood of satisfying the requirement for labour apparently becomes too uncertain and firms avoid these areas.

At the other end of the scale, FCCs, as a group, did very poorly in attracting manufacturing activity, in spite of intensity of local initiative, even when they were located in areas of high population density and were adequately situated on the provincial highway network. Partial Shopping Centres gained generally in Alberta but only gained sporadically in Manitoba and Saskatchewan. Again northern communities did better than southern communities. The inference here is that community size, too, was a constraint below a certain level.

Community Assessment of Development Initiatives

Most of the communities interviewed thought that their efforts had produced some results and most, apparently, intended to continue some or all of their efforts. All communities acknowledged, however, that a high degree of uncertainty attended their efforts, that both potential new firms and the communities attempting to help get them started faced many problems, and that competition for the few locationally mobile firms was intense. Many communities appear to have concluded that it is necessary to maintain a reasonable effort to simply stay in the game. Although successes might occur only occasionally, discontinuing all efforts would eliminate all, or nearly all, of even occasional successes.

The most popular activities with communities included business promotion, preparation of an industrial park, creation of equity funds, promotion of tourism, mentor programs, and seeking grants from senior levels of government. All had achieved some measure of success. Activities that did not generate much return included promotion in large off-Prairie cities and low-priced residential lots (for communities not adjacent to metropolitan areas).

Chapter 7: Infrastructure and Other Considerations   51

The impression gained through the interview process was that those larger communities that had developed a committed and sustained effort, including several of the options mentioned, had a better record of success than smaller communities or communities that had developed limited, low-key, or sporadic approaches.

Housing

Numerous conditions must be satisfied in order to make a potential project feasible. Requirements for infrastructure in the form of transportation, communications, energy, power, water, waste disposal, serviced land (or an existing structure) must be met in a satisfactory manner. In addition, any new economic activity implies an increase in employment, and workers need to be housed.

In the recent past, economic expansion in rural Saskatchewan has drawn on underemployed farm family members to satisfy labour requirements. Farm males and females, along with sons and daughters who might otherwise have moved away, have been recruited to staff mines, electric generators, mills, factories and hog barns in rural Saskatchewan. As long as underemployed members of farm families can be recruited, there is little or no requirement for additional housing in rural communities. Much of this potential labour force has now taken off-farm work, however. While there may still be pockets of underemployed farm labour here or there, some employers in rural Saskatchewan were trying to recruit workers from labour surplus areas elsewhere in Canada during the peak of the past boom in the mid-1990s.

When the source of local underemployed labour has been utilized, the housing question becomes important—perhaps even imposing a constraint to new project development.

Communities will normally have a stock of dwellings more or less adequate to house their current populations. Turnover will systematically produce a small percentage of vacancies. In a large community a 5 percent vacancy rate will produce a large absolute number of accommodations that could be occupied by new employees moving into the area. The same vacancy rate in a small community would produce only a small absolute number of unoccupied dwellings. Further, in a growing community, investors will usually build in anticipation of demand whereas in a stable or declining community speculative building is uncommon. Thus the potential project which requires 100 new employees might be drawn to the small subset of communities which could immediately provide accommodations even though all other requirements were met in a large number of places which lacked only the required housing.

Surveys of vacancy rates are conducted by Canada Mortgage and Housing Corporation in communities with populations of 10,000 or more. Saskatchewan Housing Corporation conducts similar surveys in communities with fewer than 10,000 population. Both surveys are of privately owned apartment buildings with three or more units. For Saskatoon and Regina, a large sample is utilized. For all other centres, all apartments of this type are surveyed. Thus the number of units surveyed also serves as a count of the stock of dwellings of this type.

In Table 27, the vacancy rates for Primary and Secondary Wholesale-Retail Centres is shown while data for the CSC, PSC, and FCC communities are provided in Table 28.

For the Wholesale-Retail centres, the vacancy rates are shown for a five-year period which reflects a cyclical pattern over the past business cycle — falling, on average, to 1999–2000 and rising thereafter. Data for the rural communities in Table 28 are for 2001 only.

A number of comparisons between the two tables are revealing. The stock of apartments (units surveyed) once again reflects the hierarchical pattern with several

Table 27
Average Vacancy Rate by City for Private Apartment Buildings of Three or More Units,
PWR and SWR Centres

Centre	Vacancy Rates by Year					Units Surveyed
	1997	1998	1999	2000	2001	
PWR						
Regina	1.5	1.7	1.4	1.4	2.1	8,623
Saskatoon	0.9	0.8	0.9	1.7	2.9	13,119
SWR						
Estevan	0.2	10.7	5.2	16.3	17.6	523
Lloydminster[1]	0.1	3.0	2.7	0.2	0.4	1,617
Moose Jaw	4.9	3.2	3.7	2.8	5.4	1,413
North Battleford	7.9	6.6	5.3	7.1	6.5	860
Prince Albert	2.2	1.9	2.5	3.2	8.0	2,373
Swift Current	0.5	2.1	5.7	6.3	5.9	759
Weyburn[2]					5.9	593
Yorkton	3.7	2.1	2.6	3.0	5.1	839

[1] For Lloydminster, 498 units in Saskatchewan, 1,119 in Alberta
[2] CMHC's survey includes communities of 10,000 population. Weyburn's population is below 10,000. The vacancy rate for 2001 is from Saskatchewan Housing Corporation's 2001 survey of communities smaller than 10,000 population.
Source: CMHC 2001 Annual Rental Market Survey.

Table 28
Average Vacancy Rate by Community for Private Apartment Buildings of Three or More Units,
CSC, PSC and FCC Centres

Centre	Vacancy Rate (%)	Units Surveyed	Centre	Vacancy Rate (%)	Units Surveyed
SWR			**FCC**		
Weyburn	5.9	593	Battleford[1]	–	–
			Big River[2]	–	–
CSC			Biggar	7.4	68
Assiniboia	7.9	38	Canora	3.7	27
Humboldt	6.7	150	Carlyle	8.6	35
Kindersley	2.2	90	Davidson	20.0	30
Meadow Lake	3.4	87	Esterhazy	25.5	102
Melfort	7.2	83	Fort Qu'Appelle	0.0	16
Melville	9.7	145	Hudson Bay	33.8	68
Nipawin	6.8	103	Indian Head	19.0	21
Tisdale	2.3	86	Kamsack	33.3	27
			Kipling[2]	–	–
PSC			Leader	31.8	22
Maple Creek	0.0	12	Lumsden[3]	–	–
Moosomin	4.9	41	Maidstone	4.8	21
Outlook	8.8	68	Oxbow	0.0	9
Rosetown	15.7	51	Redvers	13.6	22
Shaunavon	21.4	56	Shellbrook	0.0	16
Unity	11.1	18	Spiritwood[2]	–	–
			Wadena	25.0	8
			Watrous	3.1	32
			Wynyard	0.0	29

[1] Included with North Battleford
[2] Not surveyed
[3] Included with Regina
Source: Saskatchewan Housing Corporation 2001 Rental Market Survey. SHC's survey includes communities under 10,000.

thousand in Saskatoon and Regina, an average of 1,122 in SWR centres, 98 in CSCs, 41 in PSCs and 33 in FCCs.

Vacancy rates also exhibit a hierarchical relationship. Unweighted average vacancy rates are lowest in PWR Centres at 2.5 percent. For SWRs and CSCs they are 6.85 and 5.78 percent respectively. For PSCs the average vacancy rate is 10.32 percent and, for FCCs, 13.51 percent.

Thus if the average vacancy rate for SWR centres (6.85 percent) is applied to the average 1,122 apartment buildings this indicates at least 231 vacancies (if each apartment building has only three units). For FCC communities, the average vacancy rate (13.51 percent) applied to the average number of apartment buildings (33) yields 13 vacancies (at three units per apartment). While the size assumed is an understatement for both types of centres, apartment buildings would be larger in SWR communities than in FCCs. Other types of dwellings are available in each category of community, of course, with single-family detached houses being common. Larger communities would also have townhouses, duplexes, etc. Nevertheless the stock of for-rent apartments can be taken as a rough measure of the relative availability of housing throughout the hierarchy. It thus becomes apparent that housing could be the Achilles heel in considering expansion of economic activity in smaller places.

Conclusion

Infrastructure is necessary to support economic activity. But the presence of adequate infrastructure is not sufficient to ensure that economic expansion will occur. All of the 46 communities under consideration in this chapter have adequate infrastructure to support at least some types of economic expansion. But hundreds, if not thousands, of other rural communities across North America also have adequate complements of infrastructure.

Other factors then come into account. These include location relative to markets served, the *quality* of the transportation and communications systems, the size and skill mix of the labour force within commuting distance, the presence of firms in the appropriate business services categories and, as just discussed, supply of rental accommodations of sufficient size to house employees attracted from outside the area.

All of the 46 communities discussed in this chapter are capable of supporting economic expansion of some types. Circumstances favourable to expansion exist for most, if not all, sectors in centres at the top of the hierarchy. While few would want to challenge Wal-Mart head-on, the existence of other firms in the same sector generally enhances business potential by creating an agglomeration of similar or closely related activities which attract consumers interested in comparative shopping. An example of an attempt to create this type of attraction is provided by the recent relocation of many of Saskatoon's new car dealerships to a common location on Circle Drive south of the city.

The band of opportunity is not so wide in small or medium-sized communities. But for some activities, such locations may be preferred. The manufacturer who does not require much in terms of service sector support may find lower land costs, lower wages and lower taxes in a less urban setting. The greatest potential for new activity in small and medium-sized communities is in manufacturing activities with such requirements. Conventional activities in the trade and service sectors beyond what is required to satisfy local needs, are much less likely candidates because such attempts are in direct competition with the large and growing agglomerations in the major cities. Any such activities in the smaller centres need to be *complementary* with what is offered in the major cities rather than *competitive*. The spa in Watrous is an example, as are some specialized dining establishments within commuting distance of a larger centre.

Local initiative can help to facilitate this process, and may, from time to time, attract a firm which is looking for a site to set up a producing activity. For most smaller places, however, it is unlikely that local initiative can alter the process in any fundamental way.

CHAPTER 8

Functional Economic Areas

For several decades employment has shifted away from agriculture and resource-based industries towards the services and trade sectors. As part of this process, the sphere of dominance of the cities and larger rural communities has extended while the influence of smaller communities has contracted. As higher-order functions shifted to fewer and larger communities, the shopping trips of rural dwellers became longer and an ever-larger share of their expenditure was made in larger places, thus reinforcing the consolidation process.

During this same time frame, farm families have come to increasingly depend on non-farm employment to sustain their incomes. In 1967 farm families earned 75 percent of their farm household income as net farm self-employment income. By 1981 this source contributed 58 percent and, in 1996, only 31 percent of farm household income. Nonfarm household income rose, meanwhile, from 13 percent in 1967 to 21 percent in 1981 and 54 percent in 1996 (Stabler and Olfert 2000). The nonfarm employment income is earned primarily from jobs in the larger rural communities and in the province's major centres.

As rural and urban continue to integrate, the distinction blurs and the concept of community takes on a new meaning. In the past, the community was the town or village in which one lived. It was largely also the same place where employment, schools, health services, and other commercial services were routinely available. For some communities that may still be the case.

If community is defined in a functional sense, however, the definition has to evolve as changing tastes and technologies redefine what people do, how they do it, and more importantly for this issue, where it is done.

If the concept of community is to have any functional meaning, it must be defined in such a way that it encompasses the entire area within which people live, work, shop for everyday goods and services, go to school through grade 12, obtain routine medical services, and find much of their recreation and entertainment. If this is the case, the geographic area that is a functional community extends well beyond the confines of the home town. Instead of being points on a map, communities become regions that are functionally defined by their ability to serve the needs of the resident populations. Described in this way, a community might alternatively be defined as a functional economic area.

Functional Economic Areas

Conceptually, there are many ways to define functional economic areas. Two concepts that have proven useful in the context of the research reported here are the trade areas that reflect the shopping patterns of rural dwellers, and the journeys to work that delimit labour market areas. For places below the Primary Wholesale-Retail level, the two overlap to a considerable extent. Focal points of functional economic areas necessarily include one or more cities or towns that provide many of the core services required to serve the economic and social needs of the population within and adjacent to the focal point. Smaller towns, villages, and rural areas supply much of the labour that is required to perform the services provided in the focal point. Each place is complementary to every other place within the functional economic area.

Shopping Patterns

Studies of shopping habits of Saskatchewan's rural residents, conducted over a 45-year period (Saskatchewan 1957; Stabler and Williams 1974; Stabler and Olfert 1991), reveal a pattern of increasing dependence on communities at the upper levels of the hierarchy.

In 1991, the year of the last survey, a pattern had emerged in which common everyday goods and services such as elementary schools, high schools, gasoline, routine banking, and groceries were obtained in the vicinity of the rural dwellers' residence. Goods and services provided by establishments performing middle and higher order functions were purchased in either the larger regional centres or in the province's major cities (a complete discussion of the identification of the retail trade areas is found in Stabler and Olfert 1992).

Geographically, the shopping patterns of rural dwellers living near Minimum Convenience Centres was observed to be three-tiered: 28 percent of consumption expenditures were made in MCCs, 13 percent in PSCs, and 45 percent in one of the 10 largest centres (SWR and PWR). For people living elsewhere, the pattern was two-tiered with a rising percentage of consumption expenditures made in the community of residence (with ascending trade centre status of the home community) and the balance in one of the 10 major centres. Bypassing of opportunities to purchase, en route to higher level centres, was common and occurred at all lower and intermediate levels in the hierarchy (Stabler and Olfert 1992, p. 39).

Table 29
Distances Travelled by Rural Dwellers to Shop by Functional Classification of Centre, 1991

Functional Classification	Average Distance (kms)
MCC	17
FCC	26
PSC	39
CSC	50
SWR	80
PWR	141

The estimated radii of retail market areas defined by rural dwellers' 1991 shopping patterns are recorded in Table 29. Though the distances recorded for shopping trips in 1991 are undoubtedly still relatively representative, several changes in the trade centre hierarchy will have modified the detail. For example, there are many fewer communities classified as PSC and FCC and many more classified as MCCs in 2001. Theoretically this would lead to a modest reduction of the market areas of the MCCs and a modest expansion of the market areas of FCCs and PSCs. In addition, Wal-Mart and other superstores had not yet arrived on the Saskatchewan scene in great numbers in 1991. Wal-Mart's appearance in PWR and SWR communities, along with the expansion of other big box retailers in the same centres, has undoubtedly extended the market areas of the 10 centres in these two top categories.

Labour Market Areas

A labour market area may be defined as an area that is large enough to contain the workplaces of most of the people who reside within it and the residences of most of the people who work within it. For larger centres the majority of the workforce, in percentage terms, will be composed of local residents. Nevertheless, major centres provide a large absolute number of jobs for rural dwellers, and their influence extends farthest into rural space. Such centres are the "focal points" of their labour market areas. For small communities, in-commuters may make up half or more of the centre's workforce, but the absolute number of jobs provided per community is smaller than in the case of large communities. Complete labour market studies for Saskatchewan have been conducted for 1981, 1991 and 1996 (a thorough discussion of the methodology and derivation of labour market areas for Saskatchewan is found in Stabler, Olfert, and Greuel 1996; Stabler and Olfert 2000).

Data from the census on place-of-work and place-of-residence was acquired from Statistics Canada as a special tabulation of the Census of Population at the Consolidated Census Subdivision (CSD) level. *Potential* labour market focal points were identified by using the communities in the top four functional categories of the trade centre hierarchy. Second, the portions of the 900 plus CSDs *other than the focal points* were first aggregated into Rural Municipalities (RMs). Each RM was then attached to one of the potential focal points based on commuting flows.

If all the RMs could be unambiguously attached to only one of the potential focal points, the number of unique LMAs would be equal to the number of potential focal points. In some cases, however, commuting patterns are sufficiently complex (for rural geographies situated near to or between adjacent urban centres) that unequivocal assignment is not possible. To resolve the assignment, a factor analysis program was used to "pair" urban centres that share commuters in a substantial way. Urban centres that interact with the same rural space are thus paired creating a single, composite focal point where two (or more) had been hypothesized. Through this process the number of focal points will be reduced from the number initially hypothesized to a smaller number of more or less unique, self-contained focal points. As it turned out, only the top three tiers in the trade centre hierarchy formed the dominant focal points. Partial Shopping Centres (fourth tier) were simply too small to have an effective influence on spatial employment patterns.

The final step in defining the spatial structure of LMAs is achieved by using a cluster analysis program to assign rural municipalities to the set of (composite) focal points. The cluster algorithm will assign rural geographies to focal points based upon the strength of the commuting flows. Clusters are formed by creating successively larger groups, beginning with those entities most closely associated. This process will continue until it is no longer possible to form additional linkages.

Identifying Functional Economic Areas

A functional economic area (FEA) is an area that is relatively closed or bounded with respect to the income-producing activities of its residents. It is also relatively closed with respect to a cluster of everyday consumer-oriented business outlets and common public services. Almost all the labour resident in the area is employed within the area and most of the everyday goods and services consumed in the area are purchased within its boundaries. Similarly most of the K-12 student population living in the area attends school within the area and most of its residents obtain routine health and medical care within the area.[11]

---

11. The notion of functional economic areas was originally introduced by Fox and Kumar, 1965.

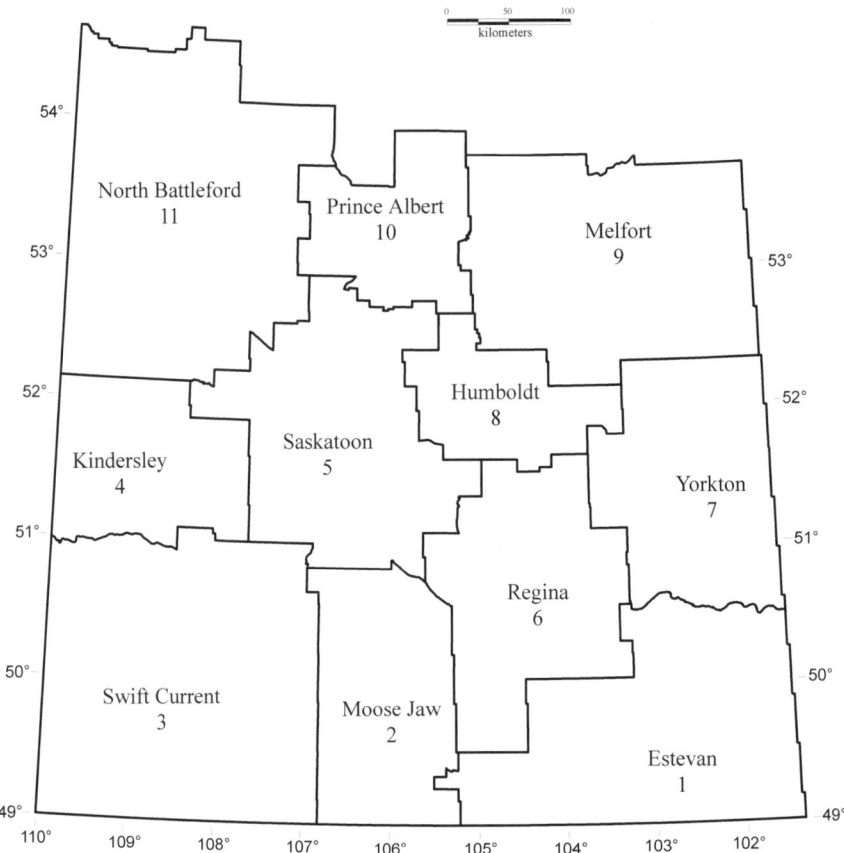

Figure 3. 11-Region Functional Economic Areas, Saskatchewan.

Functional Economic Areas were identified for Saskatchewan using the previously defined labour markets and retail trade areas. The objective was to identify FEAs which fit the criteria discussed above and also to define the FEAs in such a way that each contains areas of future population and job growth, thus ensuring the future functional viability of the specific geographies defined.[12]

Identification of FEAs was a three-step process: first, labour market areas were defined and their boundaries identified based upon labour commutes to employment centres; second, retail trade areas were superimposed over the labour market areas which assisted in assigning RMs on the boundary of two labour markets to one area or the other; and, finally, some minor adjustments were made to account for physical features such as rivers and road networks, or to reduce irregularities in the shapes of the FEAs. Through this process, an 11-region system of FEAs was defined based on the province's larger communities and including the rural space tributary to these centres for employment, shopping and public service. In this system, 9 of the FEAs have populations of 49,000 or more. Figure 3 is a map of the FEAs that were defined in this manner.

---

12. A complete discussion of the development of FEAs for Saskatchewan is found in Stabler and Olfert, 2000.

Chapter 8: Functional Economic Areas

FEAs vary in geographic size and in population. This is a reflection of the size of the FEA's largest community, the rural population density, the road network, and physical features. Nevertheless the FEAs that emerged are entities defined by the conscious choices of Saskatchewan people. They are not theoretical concepts imposed on a map of the province without regard to people's behaviour.

Characteristics of the 11-Region System

In Table 30, the population of the 11 FEAs is shown for 1998.[13] Even with substantial geographic aggregation, population size differs significantly between the smallest FEA (Kindersley) and the largest (Saskatoon). Nevertheless, even the FEAs with the smallest populations contain at least one community of CSC or higher status.

Table 30
Population[1] by 11-Region Functional Economic Areas, 1998

Functional Economic Area, Major Centre(s)	1998 Population # of people	% of province
FEA 1, Estevan-Weyburn	69,940	7.02
FEA 2, Moose Jaw	54,323	5.45
FEA 3, Swift Current	50,415	5.06
FEA 4, Kindersley-Rosetown	21,641	2.17
FEA 5, Saskatoon	267,178	26.81
FEA 6, Regina	238,850	23.96
FEA 7, Yorkton-Melville	62,826	6.30
FEA 8, Humboldt	27,432	2.75
FEA 9, Melfort-Tisdale-Nipawin	46,741	4.69
FEA 10, Prince Albert	67,246	6.75
FEA 11, North Battleford-Lloydminster	90,150	9.04
TOTAL	996,742	100.00

[1] Excludes the population of the Northern Administrative District (Census Division 18).
Source: Saskatchewan Health. Covered Population.

Commuting data, which enumerate the total number of workers resident in the FEA who commute to a job either within the FEA or to a destination beyond the FEA, were obtained for each area. A commuter's place of residence is identified as either one of the FEA's larger communities or a rural municipality (all locations other than the focal point communities which are the primary places of employment). Workplace destinations include one of the FEA's focal point communities, another RM within the FEA, or outside the FEA. Non-FEA destinations are further divided into other larger Saskatchewan focal points, other RMs and out-of-province. As shown in Table 31, the number of commuters originating in the 11 FEAs totalled 91,185 in 1996, approximately 20 percent of the province's employed labour force in that year. Several other useful observations are possible from this table. For example, the percentage of commutes originating within an FEA that also terminated in the same FEA (68,160) was equal to 75 percent of all commutes. Of these 68,160 commutes, 68 percent (46,655) were to an urban community within the same FEA while 32 percent were to a rural location. The dependence of rural dwellers on urban-based employment is even more striking. More than 82 percent (43,850) of the internal (same FEA) commutes made by rural dwellers was to a job in an urban centre. A higher percentage, but significantly smaller number, of commutes made by urban dwellers was to a rural job in the same FEA (12,165). These are school teachers, nurses, potash miners, pulp mill and oil field workers commuting from their residence in a larger centre to a job in a small town or village or in an unincorporated rural setting.

---
13. Saskatchewan Health Covered Population data, used to construct this table, do not have the problems at a macro-geographic scale that they do at a micro scale. See the discussion in Chapter 3.

Table 31
Commuting Flow Summary—All FEAs, 1996[1]

Place of Residence of Commuters	Place of Work of Commuters						
	Communities	RMs	Regional Total	Other Sask. Communities	Other SK RMs	Out of prov.	SUM
Communities	2,805	12,165	14,970	5,310	2,375	5,910	28,565
RMs	43,850	9,340	53,190	3,810	2,440	3,180	62,620
Regional Sum	46,655	21,505	68,160	9,120	4,815	9,090	91,185

[1] The set of communities used for the analysis of commuting patterns includes 62 of the province's largest centres—the set that made up the top four tiers in the trade-centre system as of 1990.

Source: Statistics Canada. 1996 Census of Population, special tabulations.

In terms of shopping patterns, the spatial configuration of the FEAs ensures that as much of the area-wide consumption spending as possible is captured within the FEA. Each FEA contains at least one Complete Shopping Centre. From the previous discussion on spatial multipliers, it can be concluded that an FEA with a CSC as its largest community would capture approximately 75 percent of the consumption expenditures made by residents of the FEA. FEAs with SWR or PWR communities would retain a higher percentage. The 11-region system identified in Figure 3 defines a system of regional economies which are as close to being self-contained as possible.

Conclusions with Respect to FEAs

Saskatchewan's rural economy has been restructuring for more than 60 years. Farms consolidated into fewer and larger units because improvements in technology and falling commodity prices compelled high land-to-labour and capital-to-labour ratios. Throughout the period small communities declined, as most commercial and some public activities moved to larger and fewer rural towns and cities. Into the 1970s, however, farmers were still primarily farmers — earning most of their family income as net farm income.

From the mid-1980s on, the process has changed. Farmers continued to consolidate as real grain prices edged ever downward and as the federal and provincial governments tried to withdraw from the process of competitive subsidization. Farm families (and other rural dwellers) came to depend increasingly on employment in the cities and larger rural towns. Rural and urban Saskatchewan have become integrated as never before through commuting to a few larger centres for employment, to shop and to access public services.

The economic environment has changed in other ways as well. The world continues to move, slowly but perhaps irreversibly, toward much freer trade. Current discussions suggest that much of Latin America may join the existing trade arrangement with Canada, Mexico and the United States.

Provincial and federal governments managed to end a decade of staggering deficits during the buoyant years of the 1990s. But in the process, underfunding of health, higher education, and other programs created in the 1960s and 1970s brought new crises. The provincial budget was balanced by allowing a substantial portion of the province's infrastructure to dramatically erode away. The year 2001 brought recession and threatened the balanced budgets thus achieved. Multibillion dollar program and infrastructure spending backlogs confront governments along with unpaid debts, new demands, and taxpayers who have wearied of the "temporary" burdens imposed to eliminate deficits. The fiscal situation of governments at all levels implies that serious prioritization and rationing will characterize public expenditure into the foreseeable future. Provincial policies which continue to support small, fragmented, and dispersed governments, institutions and infrastructure which were appropriate at the beginning of the 20th century must be seriously reevaluated.

De facto economic regions have emerged within the province. We have defined these regions based on employment and shopping behaviour of their residents. These regions, referred to as Functional Economic Areas, provide a framework within which to plan for public and private initiatives. At the centre of each is a city or larger rural community. The centre provides jobs, trade and services, both public and private. The rural areas tributary to the centres provide labour and a market for a substantial portion of the centre's business outlets and public services (Olfert and Stabler 2000).

As awareness of these regions spreads, it makes sense to support them by formally recognizing them and empowering them to plan for economic development and the inevitable future consolidations, as well as facilitating cooperation, partnerships, and alliances of the separate public and private entities within them.

CHAPTER 9

Conclusions

In this report, the evolution of Saskatchewan's trade centre system has been traced for the 40 years between 1961 and 2001. The pattern throughout this period has been one of consolidation. Population has moved from rural to urban Saskatchewan, reducing the potential market size in rural space. Rural dwellers further diminished rural demand by extending the distance travelled for shopping trips as intercity highways improved. As local market potential fell below the demand thresholds required to support middle- and upper-middle-order functions, these functions disappeared in small and medium-sized centres and expanded in larger rural towns and in the cities. In the 1990s, a variety of big box retailers, locating in Primary and Secondary Wholesale Centres, dramatically enhanced the attraction of these communities.

By 2001 the structure of the trade centre system included 18 communities in the top three functional classifications and 580 in the bottom three. The 18 centres in the top three categories dominate the hierarchy in terms of retail trade, manufacturing, public services and as employment centres that provide the vast majority of jobs for rural commuters. The future viability of the Saskatchewan economy depends upon the viability of these 18 communities.

At the other end of the spectrum, the 502 communities in the lowest category no longer play any meaningful role in the trade centre system. There is no single function of any type that is common to this set of communities. They will continue as communities only as long as people are content to live in them and commute elsewhere to work, to shop, and to obtain public services.

The remaining 78 communities include six Partial Shopping Centres (PSCs) and 72 Full Convenience Centres (FCCs). The six PSCs are somewhat unique among small rural communities. They are somewhat larger than other communities in the bottom three categories which means that their populations are large enough to satisfy the demand thresholds for several upper-middle-order functions. They are also separated by approximately an hour's driving time from any community in the top three functional categories. Thus, while their residents undoubtedly shop in the major cities, they do so less frequently than if they were only 30 minutes away from the larger centre.

The 72 FCCs divide into 22 larger centres that are almost twice the size of the 50 smaller FCCs. Their greatest relative strength is in the provision of a modest complement of middle- and low-order consumer trade and service outlets. They also offer a few producer services and have, on average, five manufacturing operations. Elementary and high schools are common and minimum health care facilities are present.

The smaller 50 FCCs are deficient in terms of producer services, producers, and infrastructure except for schools. They do, however, retain a modest complement of about a dozen low-order consumer services. Their role in rural space is somewhat like that of a 7-Eleven outlet in urban space.

Looking to the future, the communities in the top three functional categories can plan with optimism while those in the bottom category, as well as the 50 smallest FCCs, will likely continue to decline—most certainly in relative terms and probably in absolute terms as well. Only the most fortuitous of circumstances could reverse the fortunes of these 552 communities.

The six PSCs and 22 largest FCCs have retained enough population and commercial functions that they could, through good planning, good management, and good luck continue in their present roles or probably even enhance their positions somewhat. Key to their future is the presence of a sufficient supply of underemployed or unemployed labour with the requisite skills within commuting distance. In the past 15 years, new jobs in rural Saskatchewan have been filled to an extent by underemployed members of farm families. Most farm families now have one or more off-farm jobs, however. Most of this source of rural labour must now be committed. If not, when that point is reached, future expansions in rural Saskatchewan will have to attract labour from outside the immediate area.

So long as expansions of new activity could draw on a local labour force, housing was not a noticeable problem. If a labour force has to be recruited from outside the local labour market, the need for housing becomes an important consideration. Very few small communities have available a stock of housing which could accommodate an influx of even a moderate-sized labour force.

Nevertheless, if the labour and housing issues can be addressed, the PSCs and larger FCCs are capable of supporting some types of increased economic activity. Perhaps their greatest advantage lies with manufacturers who do not require much in terms of urban service sector support and would find lower land costs, lower taxes, and (to this point) somewhat lower labour costs, attractive. Such activities, serving markets across the province and beyond, would not be in head-to-head competition with manufacturers in the cities.

Other activities, in the trade and service sectors, which are complementary to those in the province's cities, are also possibilities. Unique recreational services and other unique attractions or services are potential activities for expansion.

All of the events summarized above have emphasized a continuous extension of the geographic framework within which people journey to work, shop, attend school, obtain health care and, in general, live their everyday lives. In the process the concept of community, as a functional entity, has evolved from village or town to a region large enough to satisfy the everyday requirements of rural dwellers. By extending their sphere of spatial interaction, rural people routinely bypass much of the redundant public infrastructure and institutions that are retained at considerable expense in rural Saskatchewan.

Provincial government policies continue to support a plethora of governments and infrastructure which are too small to capture economies of scale, too fragmented to realize economies of scope and too dispersed to generate agglomeration economies. Such policies ensure that trade centre decline reaches higher into the system than what would have been the case had rationalization been pursued at an earlier date. These policies have also left rural Saskatchewan with a set of institutions and infrastructure which is obsolete, cumbersome and inefficient. The existing structure of the rural system is actually an impediment to economic development. This is a very unfortunate framework within which to enter the highly competitive world of the 21st century.

Chapter 9: Conclusions

While it is late in the game, reorganization focussed on creating efficient governmental jurisdictions, institutions and infrastructure through the use new knowledge, information, communication technologies and collaborations, will do more to enhance the future of rural Saskatchewan than continuation of policies which vainly attempt to protect the past.

References

Anding, Thomas L. et al. 1990. *Trade Centers of the Upper Midwest: Changes From 1960 to 1989*. Minneapolis: Center for Urban and Regional Affairs, University of Minnesota.

Barger, Harold, and Hans Landsberg. 1942. *American Agriculture, 1899–1939: A Study of Output, Employment and Productivity*. New York: National Bureau of Economic Research.

Barkley, Andrew P., 1990. "The Determinants of the Migration of Labor Out of Agriculture in the U.S., 1940–85." *American Journal of Agricultural Economics* 72: 567–73.

Barkley, David, ed. 1993. *Economic Adaptation: Alternatives for Nonmetropolitan Areas*. Boulder, CO: Westview Press.

Barkley, David. 1996. The Economics of Change in Rural America. Department of Agricultural Economics, Clemson University, mimeo.

Barkley, David, Mark Henry, Shumming Bao, and Kerry Brooks. 1995. "How Functional are Economic Areas? Tests for Intra-regional Spatial Association Using Spatial Data Analysis." *Papers in Regional Science* 74, no. 4: 297–316.

Berry, Brian and John Parr. 1988. *Market Centers and Retail Location: Theory and Applications*. Englewood Cliffs, NJ: Prentice-Hall.

Bollman, Ray, ed. 1992. *Rural and Small Town Canada*. Ottawa: Supply and Services Canada.

Borchert, John R., and Russell B. Adams. 1963. *Trade Centers and Tributary Areas of the Upper Midwest*. Minneapolis: University of Minnesota, Upper Midwest Economic Study.

Britnell, G.E. 1939. *The Wheat Economy*. Toronto: University of Toronto Press.

Canada Mortgage and Housing Corporation. 2001. *Annual Rental Marketing Survey*.

Canadian Bar Association Saskatchewan Branch. 2000. Legal Directory and Day Planner — 2000–2001 Edition. The Canadian Bar Association, Saskatchewan Branch.

Canadian Grain Commission. 2001. Elevators Capacities and Deliveries, http://www.cgc.ca/Pubs/GrainDeliveries/deliveries-e.htm

Chandra, Amitabh and Eric Thompson. 2000. "Does Public Infrastructure Affect Economic Activity? Evidence from the Interstate Highway System." *Regional Science and Urban Economics* 30: 457–90.

College of Physicians and Surgeons of the Province of Saskatchewan. 2001. Physician Mailing List 2001.

Drabenstott, Mark, Mark Henry and Lynn Gibson. 1986. "A Changing Rural America." *Economic Review*, Federal Reserve Bank of Kansas City (July/August): 23–24.

Drabenstott, Mark, Mark Henry and Lynn Gibson. 1987. "The Rural Economic Policy Choice." *Economic Review*, Federal Reserve Bank of Kansas City (January): 4–58.

Drabenstott, Mark. 2001. "Meeting Rural America's Challenges in the 21st Century: Rethinking Rural Policy." Paper presented at the Western Regional Science Association Meetings. Palm Springs, California. February 2001.

Dun and Bradstreet. n.d. *Reference Book*. Toronto: Dun and Bradstreet, quarterly and electronic data.

Economic Research Service. 1998. *Telecommunications in Rural Areas.* Washington, DC: U.S. Department of Agriculture.

Ellison, Glenn and Edward L. Glaeser. 1997. "Geographic Concentration in U.S. Manufacturing Industries: A Dartboard Approach." *Journal of Political Economy* 105, no. 5: 889–927.

Flora, Cornelia B., and James A. Christenson, eds. 1991. *Rural Policies for the 1990s.* Boulder, CO: Westview Press.

Freshwater, David. 1997. "Farm Production Policy Versus Rural Life Policy." *American Journal of Agricultural Economics* 79, no. 5: 1515–24.

Fowke, V.C. 1957. *The National Policy and The Wheat Economy.* Toronto: University of Toronto Press.

Fox, Karl, and Krishna Kumar. 1965. "The Functional Economic Area: Delineation and Implications for Economic Analysis and Policy." *Papers of the Regional Science Association* 15: 57–84.

Furtan, W.H., and G.E. Lee. 1977. "Economic Development of the Saskatchewan Wheat Economy." *Canadian Journal of Agricultural Economics* 25: 15–28.

Gardner, Bruce. 2000. "Economic Growth and Low Incomes in Agriculture." *American Journal of Agricultural Economics* 82, no. 5: 1059–74.

Glasmeier, Amy K. and Marie Howland. 1995. *From Combines to Computers: Rural Services and Development in the Age of Information Technology.* Albany: State University of New York.

Gordon, Peter, Harry Richardson and Gang Yu. 1998. "Metropolitan and Non-Metropolitan Employment Trends in the U. S.: Recent Evidence and Implications." *Urban Studies* 35, no. 7: 1037–57.

Government of Saskatchewan. 2001. Saskatchewan Education Enrollment Statistics 2000–2001.

——. 2000. Annual Report 1999–2000.

Hill, Berkeley. 1999. "Farm Household Incomes: Perceptions and Statistics." *Journal of Rural Studies* 15 no. 3: 345–58.

Hodge, Gerald. 1965. "Trade Center Viability in the Great Plains." *Papers of the Regional Science Association* 15: 87–115.

Isserman, Andrew. 1994. "State Economic Development Policy and Practice in the United States: A Survey Article." *International Regional Science Review* 16, no. 1: 49–100.

Lepnurm, Marje. 1995. "Hospital Closures in Rural Saskatchewan: A Predictive Model." (MA thesis, University of Saskatchewan, Saskatoon)

Mackintosh, W.A. 1934. *Prairie Settlement.* Toronto: MacMillan.

Martin, Chester, and Arthur S. Morton. 1938. *History of Prairie Settlement and "Dominion Lands" Policy.* Toronto: MacMillan.

Mieszkowski, Peter and Edwin Mills. 1993. "The Causes of Metropolitan Suburbanization." *Journal of Economic Perspectives* 7, no. 3: 135–47.

Morrison, Catherine J. and Amy Schwartz. 1996. "State Infrastructure and Productive Performance." *American Economic Review* 86, no. 5: 1095–1111.

Mulligan, Gordon. 1984. "Agglomeration and Central Place Theory." *International Regional Science Review* 9: 1–42.

Nevin, Edward. 1966. "The Case for Regional Policy." *The Three Banks Review* (December): 30–46.

Olfert, M. Rose and Jack C. Stabler. 2000. "Rural Communities of the Saskatchewan Prairie Landscape." In *Prairie Forum* Special Issue: Changing Prairie Landscapes 25: 123–38.

——. 2000. "Rural Labor Force Characteristics: The Center-Periphery Continuum." Working paper. Saskatoon, SK: Department of Agricultural Economics, University of Saskatchewan.

——. 1999. "Multipliers in a Central Place Hierarchy." *Growth and Change* 30: 288–302.

——. 1998. "Spatial Dimensions of Rural, Gender Specific Labour Force Commuting Patterns." *Australasian Journal of Regional Studies* 4, no. 2: 253–74.

——. "Community Level Multipliers for Rural Development Initiatives." *Growth and Change* 25 (Fall): 467–86.

——. 1994. "Industrial Restructuring of the Prairie Labour Force: Spatial and Gender Impacts." *Canadian Journal of Regional Science* 17: 133–52.

Pezzini, Merio. 2000. "Rural Policy Lessons from OECD Countries." *Economic Review*, Federal Reserve Bank of Kansas City. 85, no. 3: 47–57.

Phillips, W.G. 1956. *The Agricultural Implements Industry in Canada.* Toronto: University of Toronto Press.

References

Porter, Michael. 1996. "Competitive Advantage, Agglomeration Economies and Regional Policy." *International Regional Science Review* 19: 85–94.

Reed, David A. 1989. *The Winnowing: Economic Change in Rural America*. New York: The Hudson Institute.

Saskatchewan. 1957. *Royal Commission on Agriculture and Rural Life. Service Centres*. Regina: Queen's Printer.

Saskatchewan Health. 1971–1998. *Covered Population*. Regina: Queen's Printer.

Saskatchewan Housing Corporation. 2001. *Rental Market Survey*.

Smith, Stephen. 1995. "The Changing Rural Policy Context." *Agriculture and Resource Economics Review* 17: 139–45.

Stabler, Jack C. 1996. "Economics and Multicommunity Partnerships." *Canadian Journal of Regional Science* 19, no. 1: 83–105.

———. 1986. "Trade Center Evolution in the Great Plains." *Journal of Regional Science* 27: 225–44.

Stabler, Jack C. and M. Rose Olfert. 2000. *Functional Economic Areas in Saskatchewan: A Framework for Municipal Restructuring*. Saskatoon: University of Saskatchewan.

———. 2000. "Public Policy in the 21st Century: Is Prairie Agriculture Becoming Like Any Other Industry? Does it Matter?" *Canadian Journal of Agricultural Economics* 48, no. 4: 385–95.

———. 1999. *Impact of the Termination of the Crow Subsidy in the Context of Economic Restructuring in the East Central Region*. Prepared for Agriculture Canada–PFRA. Saskatoon: University of Saskatchewan.

———. 1996. *The Changing Role of Rural Communities in an Urbanizing World: Saskatchewan An Update to 1995*. Regina: Canadian Plains Research Center.

———. 1994. "Multicommunity Partnerships in Rural Development: An Alberta Case Study." *Canadian Journal of Regional Science* 17: 71–94.

———. 1992. *Restructuring Rural Saskatchewan: The Challenge of the 1990s*. Regina: Canadian Plains Research Center

Stabler, Jack C., M. Rose Olfert and Jonathan Greuel. 1996. "Spatial Labor Markets and the Rural Labor Force." *Growth and Change* 27: 206–30.

Stabler, Jack C., M. R. Olfert, and Murray Fulton. 1992. *The Changing Role of Rural Communities in an Urbanizing World: Saskatchewan 1961–1990*. Regina: Canadian Plains Research Center.

Stabler, Jack C., and Peter R. Williams. 1973. *The Dynamics of a System of Central Places*. Reading, U K: University of Reading.

Statistics Canada. 1996. Censuses of Agriculture and Population. Special Tabulations.

———. 1996. Census of Population, GeoSuite.

Summers, Gene. 1993. "Rural Development Options" in David Barkley, ed., *Economic Adaptation: Alternatives for Non-metropolitan Areas*. Boulder, CO: Westview Press.

Tweeten, Luther and Carl Zulauf. 1997. "Public Policy for Agriculture After Commodity Programs." *Review of Agricultural Economics* 19, no. 2: 263–80.

Urquhart, M.C. and K.A.H. Buckley. 1965. *Historical Statistics of Canada*. Toronto: The Macmillan Company.

Wensley, M.R. and J.C. Stabler. 1998. "Demand-Threshold Estimation for Business Activities in Rural Saskatchewan." *Journal of Regional Science* 38, no. 1: 155–77.

Wionzek, Jacynthe. 1995. "Education Delivery in Rural Saskatchewan." (MSc thesis, University of Saskatchewan, Saskatoon)

Yamano, Norihiko and Toro Ohkawara. 2000. "The Regional Allocation of Public Investment: Efficiency or Equity?" *Journal of Regional Science* 40, no. 2: 205–29.

APPENDIX

List of Names of All Communities Included in the Study and Their 1961, 1981, 1990, 1995, and 2001 Status in the Trade Centre Hierarchy

Community	1961 Cluster	1981 Cluster	1990 Cluster	1995 Cluster	2001 Cluster
Abbey	2	2	1	1	1*
Aberdeen	2	2	1	1	1**
Abernethy	1	1	2	1	1*
Adanac	1	1	1	1	1*
Admiral	1	1	1	1	1*
Alameda	2	1	1	2	1*
Albertville	1	1	1	1	1**
Algrove	1	1	1	1	1*
Alida	2	1	1	1	1**
Allan	2	2	2	1	1*
Alsask	1	1	1	1	1**
Alvena	2	1	1	1	1**
Amsterdam	1	1	1	1	1*
Aneroid	2	1	1	1	1*
Antler	2	1	1	1	1*
Arborfield	3	2	2	1	1***
Archerwill	2	1	2	1	1*
Arcola	3	2	1	1	1***
Ardath	1	1	1	1	1*
Ardill	1	1	1	1	1*
Arelee	1	1	1	1	1*
Arran	2	1	1	1	1*
Asquith	2	1	1	1	1**
Assiniboia	4	4	3	3	4
Atwater	1	1	1	1	1***
Avonlea	2	2	2	1	1***
Aylesbury	2	1	1	1	1*
Aylsham	2	1	1	1	1*
Balcarres	3	2	3	2	2#
Baldwinton	1	1	1	1	1**
Balgonie	2	2	1	1	1***
Bangor	1	1	1	1	1*
Bankend	1	1	1	1	1*
Battleford	3	3	3	3	2##
Beatty	1	1	1	1	1*

1 = MCC; 2 = FCC; 3 = PSC; 4 = CSC; 5 = SWR; 6 = PWR
*** Top 72; **Middle 123; *Smallest 307; ## Top 22; # Smallest 50

Appendix, continued					
Community	1961 Cluster	1981 Cluster	1990 Cluster	1995 Cluster	2001 Cluster
Beaubier	1	1	1	1	1**
Beechy	2	2	2	1	1**
Belle Plaine	1	1	1	1	1***
Bellegarde	1	1	1	1	1*
Benson	1	1	1	1	1*
Bertwell	1	1	1	1	1*
Bethune	2	1	2	1	1**
Beverly	1	1	1	1	1*
Bienfait	3	2	1	1	1**
Big Beaver	1	1	1	1	1*
Big River	2	2	3	3	2##
Biggar	4	4	3	3	2##
Birch Hills	3	2	2	2	1***
Birsay	1	1	1	1	1**
Bladworth	1	1	1	1	1**
Blaine Lake	3	2	2	1	1**
Blumenheim	1	1	1	1	1*
Blumenhof	1	1	1	1	1*
Blumenort	1	1	1	1	1*
Blumenthal	1	1	1	1	1*
Borden	2	2	2	1	1***
Bounty	1	1	1	1	1*
Bracken	1	1	1	1	1*
Bradwell	1	1	1	1	1*
Brancepath	1	1	1	1	1*
Bredenbury	2	1	2	1	1*
Briercrest	2	1	1	1	1**
Broadview	3	3	2	2	1***
Brock	2	1	1	1	1**
Broderick	1	1	1	1	1*
Brownlee	1	1	1	1	1*
Bruno	3	2	2	1	1***
Buchanan	2	1	2	1	1*
Burstall	2	1	2	1	1**
Cabri	3	2	2	1	1***
Cadillac	2	1	1	1	1*
Calder	2	1	1	1	1*
Candiac	1	1	1	1	1*
Canora	4	4	3	3	2##
Canwood	2	2	2	2	1****
Carievale	2	1	1	1	1*
Carlton	1	1	1	1	1*
Carlyle	3	3	3	2	2##
Carmel	1	1	1	1	1*
Carnduff	3	3	3	2	2#
Caron	1	1	1	1	1**
Carragana	2	1	1	1	1*
Carrot River	3	3	2	2	2#
Cedoux	1	1	1	1	1*
Central Butte	3	2	2	1	1***
Ceylon	2	1	1	1	1**
Chamberlain	2	1	1	1	1**
Chaplin	2	1	1	1	1**
Chelan	1	1	1	1	1*
Chitek Lake	1	1	1	1	1*
Choiceland	2	2	2	1	1***
Chortitz	1	1	1	1	1*
Churchbridge	2	2	2	1	1***

1 = MCC; 2 = FCC; 3 = PSC; 4 = CSC; 5 = SWR; 6 = PWR
*** Top 72; **Middle 123; *Smallest 307; ## Top 22; # Smallest 50

Appendix

Appendix, continued

Community	1961 Cluster	1981 Cluster	1990 Cluster	1995 Cluster	2001 Cluster
Clair	1	1	1	1	1**
Claybank	1	1	1	1	1*
Climax	3	2	2	1	1***
Cochin	1	1	1	1	1**
Coderre	2	1	1	1	1**
Codette	1	2	1	1	1*
Coleville	2	1	2	1	1**
Colgate	1	1	1	1	1*
Collacott Subd.	1	1	1	1	1*
Colonsay	2	2	2	1	1*
Congress	1	1	1	1	1*
Conquest	2	1	1	1	1*
Consul	2	1	1	1	1*
Corning	1	1	1	1	1*
Coronach	2	2	2	1	2#
Courval	1	1	1	1	1*
Craik	3	2	2	1	1***
Crane Valley	1	1	1	1	1*
Craven	1	1	1	1	1**
Creelman	2	1	2	1	1*
Crooked River	1	1	1	1	1*
Crutwell	1	1	1	1	1*
Crystal Springs	1	1	1	1	1*
Cudworth	3	3	3	2	2#
Cupar	3	2	2	1	1***
Cut Knife	3	2	2	2	2#
Dafoe	1	1	1	1	1*
Dalmeny	2	2	2	2	2#
Danbury	1	1	1	1	1*
Darcy	1	1	1	1	1*
Davidson	3	3	3	3	2##
Davin	1	1	1	1	1*
Debden	2	2	2	1	2#
Delisle	3	2	2	1	1***
Delmas	1	1	1	1	1*
Demaine	1	1	1	1	1*
Denholm	1	1	1	1	1*
Denzil	2	1	1	1	1***
Dilke	1	1	1	1	1*
Dinsmore	3	2	2	1	1***
Disley	1	1	1	1	1*
Dodsland	3	2	2	1	1**
Dollard	1	1	1	1	1*
Domremy	2	2	1	1	1**
Dorintosh	1	1	1	1	1*
Drake	2	1	1	1	1*
Drinkwater	1	1	1	1	1*
Dubuc	2	1	1	1	1*
Duck Lake	2	2	2	2	1***
Duff	2	1	1	1	1*
Dunblane	1	1	1	1	1*
Dundurn	2	1	1	1	1**
Duval	2	1	1	1	1*
Dysart	2	1	2	1	1**
Earl Grey	2	1	1	1	1**
Eastend	3	2	2	2	2#
Eatonia	3	2	2	2	1***
Ebenezer	1	1	1	1	1***

1 = MCC; 2 = FCC; 3 = PSC; 4 = CSC; 5 = SWR; 6 = PWR
*** Top 72; **Middle 123; *Smallest 307; ## Top 22; # Smallest 50

Appendix, continued					
Community	1961 Cluster	1981 Cluster	1990 Cluster	1995 Cluster	2001 Cluster
Edam	2	2	2	1	1***
Edenwold	2	1	1	1	1*
Edgeley	1	1	1	1	1*
Elbow	2	1	1	1	1**
Elfros	1	1	1	1	1*
Elrose	3	2	2	2	2#
Elstow	2	1	1	1	1*
Endeavour	1	1	1	1	1**
Englefeld	1	2	1	1	1**
Ernfold	1	1	1	1	1*
Erwood	1	1	1	1	1*
Esk	1	1	1	1	1*
Esterhazy	4	4	3	3	2##
Estevan	5	5	5	5	5
Eston	4	3	3	2	2#
Evesham	1	1	1	1	1*
Eyebrow	2	1	1	1	1*
Fairholme	1	1	1	1	1*
Fairlight	2	1	1	1	1*
Fairy Glen	1	1	1	1	1*
Fenwood	1	1	1	1	1*
Fielding	1	1	1	1	1*
Fife Lake	2	1	1	1	1*
Fillmore	2	2	2	2	2#
Findlater	1	1	1	1	1*
Fir Mountain	1	1	1	1	1*
Fiske	1	1	1	1	1*
Flaxcombe	1	1	1	1	1*
Fleming	2	1	1	1	1**
Foam Lake	3	3	3	3	2#
Forgan	1	1	1	1	1*
Forget	1	1	1	1	1*
Fort Qu'Appelle	4	4	3	2	2##
Fox Valley	2	2	2	1	1***
Francis	2	1	1	1	1*
Frenchman Butte	1	1	1	1	1*
Frobisher	2	1	1	1	1*
Frontier	2	2	2	1	1***
Fulda	1	1	1	1	1*
Furdale	1	1	1	1	1*
Gainsborough	3	2	2	1	1***
Garrick	1	1	1	1	1*
Gerald	1	1	1	1	1**
Girvin	1	1	1	1	1*
Glaslyn	2	2	2	1	1***
Glen Ewen	2	1	1	1	1**
Glenavon	2	2	1	1	1**
Glenbain	1	1	1	1	1*
Glenbush	1	1	1	1	1*
Glenside	1	1	1	1	1*
Glentworth	2	1	1	1	1*
Glidden	1	1	1	1	1*
Golden Prairie	2	1	1	1	1*
Goodeve	2	1	1	1	1*
Goodsoil	2	2	1	1	1***
Goodwater	1	1	1	1	1*
Gorlitz	1	1	1	1	1*
Govan	3	2	1	1	1**

1 = MCC; 2 = FCC; 3 = PSC; 4 = CSC; 5 = SWR; 6 = PWR
*** Top 72; **Middle 123; *Smallest 307; ## Top 22; # Smallest 50

Appendix, continued

Community	1961 Cluster	1981 Cluster	1990 Cluster	1995 Cluster	2001 Cluster
Grand Coulee	1	1	1	1	1*
Gravelbourg	4	3	3	2	2#
Gray	1	1	1	1	1*
Grayson	2	1	1	1	1**
Greenfield	1	1	1	1	1*
Grenfell	3	3	3	2	2#
Griffin	1	1	1	1	1*
Gronlid	1	1	1	1	1*
Gruenthal	1	1	1	1	1*
Guernsey	1	1	1	1	1*
Gull Lake	4	3	3	2	2#
Hafford	3	2	2	2	1***
Hagen	1	1	1	1	1*
Hague	2	2	2	1	1***
Halbrite	1	1	1	1	1*
Handel	1	1	1	1	1*
Hanley	2	2	2	1	1**
Hardy	1	1	1	1	1*
Harris	2	2	1	1	1**
Hawarden	2	1	1	1	1*
Hazel Dell	1	1	1	1	1*
Hazenmore	1	1	1	1	1*
Hendon	1	1	1	1	1*
Henribourg	1	1	1	1	1*
Hepburn	2	2	1	1	1**
Herbert	3	3	2	2	2#
Herschel	1	1	1	1	1*
Heward	1	1	1	1	1*
Hitchcock	1	1	1	1	1*
Hodgeville	2	2	2	1	1***
Hoey	1	1	1	1	1*
Holdfast	2	1	1	1	1**
Hubbard	2	1	1	1	1*
Hudson Bay	3	4	3	3	2##
Humboldt	4	4	4	4	4
Hyas	2	1	1	1	1*
Imperial	3	2	2	1	1***
Indian Head	4	3	3	3	2##
Insinger	1	1	1	1	1*
Invermay	3	2	2	2	1***
Ituna	3	3	2	2	2#
Jansen	2	1	1	1	1*
Jasmin	1	1	1	1	1*
Jedburgh	2	1	1	1	1*
Kamsack	4	4	3	3	2##
Kayville	1	1	1	1	1*
Keeler	1	1	1	1	1*
Kelfield	1	1	1	1	1*
Kelliher	2	2	1	1	1*
Kelvington	3	3	3	2	2#
Kenaston	2	2	2	1	1***
Kendal	1	1	1	1	1**
Kennedy	2	1	1	1	1**
Kenosee Lake	1	1	1	1	1*
Kerrobert	4	3	2	2	2#
Khedive	1	1	1	1	1*
Killaly	2	1	2	1	1**
Kincaid	3	2	1	1	1***

1 = MCC; 2 = FCC; 3 = PSC; 4 = CSC; 5 = SWR; 6 = PWR
*** Top 72; **Middle 123; *Smallest 307; ## Top 22; # Smallest 50

Appendix, continued					
Community	1961 Cluster	1981 Cluster	1990 Cluster	1995 Cluster	2001 Cluster
Kindersley	4	4	4	4	4
Kinistino	3	2	2	2	2##
Kinley	1	1	1	1	1*
Kipling	3	3	3	2	2#
Kisbey	2	1	1	1	1**
Kronau	1	1	1	1	1*
Krydor	2	1	1	1	1*
Kurocki	1	1	1	1	1*
Kyle	3	2	2	1	1***
Lac Vert	1	1	1	1	1*
Lacadena	1	1	1	1	1*
Lafleche	3	2	2	1	2#
Laird	1	1	1	1	1*
Lajord	1	1	1	1	1*
Lake Alma	2	1	1	1	1*
Lake Lenore	2	2	1	1	1**
Lampman	3	2	2	1	2#
Lancer	1	1	1	1	1**
Landis	2	2	1	1	1**
Lang	2	1	1	1	1**
Langbank	1	1	1	1	1*
Langenburg	3	3	3	2	2#
Langham	2	2	2	2	1**
Lanigan	3	3	3	2	2#
Laporte	1	1	1	1	1*
Lashburn	3	2	2	1	1***
Laura	1	1	1	1	1*
Lawson	1	1	1	1	1*
Leader	4	3	2	2	2##
Leask	2	2	2	2	1***
Leipzig	1	1	1	1	1*
Lemberg	3	2	1	1	1***
Lemsford	1	1	1	1	1*
Leoville	2	2	2	1	1***
Leross	2	1	1	1	1**
Leroy	2	1	2	1	1***
Leslie	1	1	1	1	1*
Lestock	2	2	1	1	1***
Liberty	2	1	1	1	1*
Limerick	2	1	1	1	1*
Lintlaw	2	1	1	1	1**
Lipton	3	2	1	1	1***
Lisieux	1	1	1	1	1**
Livelong	1	1	2	1	1***
Lloydminster	5	5	5	5	5
Lockwood	1	1	1	1	1*
Lone Rock	1	1	1	1	1*
Loon Lake	2	2	2	2	1***
Loreburn	2	2	1	1	1*
Lorlie	1	1	1	1	1*
Love	1	1	1	1	1**
Loverna	1	1	1	1	1**
Lucky Lake	3	2	2	2	1***
Lumsden	2	2	2	2	2##
Luseland	3	2	2	1	2#
Macdowall	1	1	1	1	1*
Macklin	3	2	3	2	2#
MacNutt	2	1	1	1	1*

1 = MCC; 2 = FCC; 3 = PSC; 4 = CSC; 5 = SWR; 6 = PWR
*** Top 72; **Middle 123; *Smallest 307; ## Top 22; # Smallest 50

Appendix

Appendix, continued					
Community	1961 Cluster	1981 Cluster	1990 Cluster	1995 Cluster	2001 Cluster
Macoun	1	1	1	1	1*
Macrorie	1	1	1	1	1**
Madison	1	1	1	1	1*
Maidstone	3	2	3	2	2##
Major	2	1	1	1	1*
Manitou Beach	1	1	1	1	1*
Mankota	3	2	2	1	1***
Manor	2	2	1	1	1**
Mantario	1	1	1	1	1*
Maple Creek	4	4	3	3	3
Marcelin	2	1	1	1	1**
Marchwell	1	1	1	1	1*
Marengo	1	1	1	1	1*
Margo	2	1	1	1	1*
Markinch	1	1	1	1	1*
Marquis	1	1	1	1	1*
Marsden	2	2	1	1	1**
Marshall	1	1	1	1	1**
Maryfield	3	2	2	1	1***
Mayfair	1	1	1	1	1*
Maymont	2	1	1	1	1*
Mazenod	2	1	1	1	1*
McCord	1	1	1	1	1*
McKague	1	1	1	1	1*
McTaggart	1	1	1	1	1*
Meacham	2	1	1	1	1**
Meadow Lake	4	4	4	4	4
Meath Park	2	1	2	1	1**
Medstead	2	1	1	1	1**
Meleval	1	1	1	1	1*
Melfort	4	4	4	4	4
Melville	4	4	3	4	4
Mendham	2	1	1	1	1*
Meota	1	1	1	1	1**
Mervin	2	1	1	1	1*
Meskanaw	1	1	1	1	1*
Meyronne	1	1	1	1	1*
Midale	3	2	2	2	2#
Mikado	1	1	1	1	1*
Milden	3	2	2	1	1**
Milestone	2	2	2	1	1***
Montmartre	3	2	2	1	1**
Moose Jaw	5	5	5	5	5
Moosomin	4	4	3	3	3
Morse	2	2	1	1	1**
Mortlach	1	1	1	1	1**
Mossbank	3	2	2	1	1***
Mozart	1	1	1	1	1**
Muenster	2	1	1	1	1**
Naicam	3	2	2	1	2#
Neidpath	1	1	1	1	1*
Neilburg	3	2	2	1	2#
Netherhill	1	1	1	1	1*
Neuanlage	1	1	1	1	1*
Neudorf	3	1	1	1	1***
Neuhorst	1	1	1	1	1*
Neville	2	1	1	1	1*
Nipawin	4	4	4	4	4

1 = MCC; 2 = FCC; 3 = PSC; 4 = CSC; 5 = SWR; 6 = PWR
*** Top 72; **Middle 123; *Smallest 307; ## Top 22; # Smallest 50

Appendix, continued					
Community	1961 Cluster	1981 Cluster	1990 Cluster	1995 Cluster	2001 Cluster
Nokomis	3	2	2	1	2 #
Norquay	3	2	2	2	1 *
North Battleford	5	5	5	5	5
North Portal	1	1	1	1	1 **
Northside	1	1	1	1	1 *
Nut Mountain	1	1	1	1	1 *
Odessa	2	1	1	1	1 **
Ogema	2	2	2	1	1***
Ormistan	1	1	1	1	1 *
Osage	1	1	1	1	1 *
Oungre	1	1	1	1	1 *
Outlook	4	4	3	3	3
Oxbow	3	3	3	2	2 ##
Paddockwood	2	1	1	1	1 **
Palmer	1	1	1	1	1 *
Pambrun	1	1	1	1	1 *
Pangman	2	2	2	1	1 **
Paradise Hill	2	2	2	1	1***
Parkbeg	1	1	1	1	1 *
Parkerview	1	1	1	1	1 *
Parkside	1	1	1	1	1 *
Parry	1	1	1	1	1 *
Pathlow	1	1	1	1	1*
Paynton	1	1	1	1	1**
Peerless	1	1	1	1	1*
Pelly	2	2	1	1	1*
Pennant	2	1	1	1	1*
Pense	1	1	1	1	1**
Penzance	1	1	1	1	1*
Perdue	2	2	2	1	1**
Perigord	1	1	1	1	1*
Peterson	1	1	1	1	1*
Piapot	2	1	1	1	1*
Plato	1	1	1	1	1*
Pleasant Heights	1	1	1	1	1*
Pleasantdale	1	1	1	1	1**
Plenty	2	2	1	1	1**
Plunkett	1	1	1	1	1*
Ponteix	3	3	2	2	2 #
Porcupine Plain	3	2	2	2	2 #
Portreeve	1	1	1	1	1*
Prairie River	1	1	1	1	1**
Preeceville	3	3	3	2	2 #
Prelate	2	1	1	1	1*
Primate	1	1	1	1	1*
Prince Albert	5	5	5	5	5
Prud'Homme	2	2	1	1	1*
Punnichy	3	2	2	1	1***
Qu'Appelle	3	2	1	1	1***
Quill Lake	3	2	1	1	1***
Quinton	2	1	1	1	1***
Rabbit Lake	2	2	2	1	1*
Radisson	3	2	2	1	1***
Radville	3	2	2	1	2 #
Rama	2	1	1	1	1*
Raymore	2	2	3	1	2 #
Red Wing Terrace	1	1	1	1	1*
Redvers	3	2	3	2	2 ##

1 = MCC; 2 = FCC; 3 = PSC; 4 = CSC; 5 = SWR; 6 = PWR
*** Top 72; **Middle 123; *Smallest 307; ## Top 22; # Smallest 50

Appendix

Appendix, continued

Community	1961 Cluster	1981 Cluster	1990 Cluster	1995 Cluster	2001 Cluster
Regina	6	6	6	6	6
Regina Beach	2	2	1	1	1***
Reward	1	1	1	1	1*
Rhein	2	1	1	1	1*
Rheinland	1	1	1	1	1*
Rhineland	1	1	1	1	1*
Riceton	1	1	1	1	1*
Richard	1	1	1	1	1*
Richlea	1	1	1	1	1*
Richmound	2	1	2	1	1**
Ridgedale	2	1	1	1	1**
Riverhurst	3	1	1	1	1**
Riverside	1	1	1	1	1*
Robsart	1	1	1	1	1*
Rocanville	3	2	2	1	2#
Roche Percee	1	1	1	1	1*
Rockglen	3	2	2	1	2#
Rockhaven	1	1	1	1	1*
Rose Valley	3	2	2	1	1***
Rosenhaf	1	1	1	1	1*
Rosetown	4	4	3	3	3
Rosthern	3	3	3	2	2#
Rouleau	2	2	1	1	1***
Ruddell	1	1	1	1	1*
Runnymede	1	1	1	1	1*
Rush Lake	1	1	1	1	1*
Ruthilda	1	1	1	1	1*
Saltcoats	2	1	1	1	1**
Salvador	1	1	1	1	1*
Saskatoon	6	6	6	6	6
Sceptre	2	1	1	1	1*
Schoenfeld	1	1	1	1	1*
Scott	1	1	1	1	1*
Scout Lake	1	1	1	1	1*
Sedley	1	1	1	1	1**
Semans	3	2	1	1	1**
Senlac	2	1	1	1	1**
Shackleton	1	1	1	1	1*
Shamrock	2	1	1	1	1*
Shaunavon	4	4	3	3	3
Sheho	2	1	1	1	1*
Shell Lake	2	1	1	1	1**
Shellbrook	3	3	3	3	2##
Silton	1	1	1	1	1**
Simmie	1	1	1	1	1**
Simpson	2	1	1	1	1**
Smeaton	2	1	2	1	1**
Smiley	2	1	1	1	1**
Snowden	1	1	1	1	1*
Somme	1	1	1	1	1**
Sonningdale	1	1	1	1	1**
Southey	3	2	2	1	2#
Sovereign	1	1	1	1	1*
Spalding	3	1	2	1	1***
Speers	2	1	1	1	1*
Spiritwood	3	3	3	3	2##
Spring Valley	1	1	1	1	1*
Spring Water	1	1	1	1	1*

1 = MCC; 2 = FCC; 3 = PSC; 4 = CSC; 5 = SWR; 6 = PWR
*** Top 72; **Middle 123; *Smallest 307; ## Top 22; # Smallest 50

Appendix, continued					
Community	1961 Cluster	1981 Cluster	1990 Cluster	1995 Cluster	2001 Cluster
Springfield	1	1	1	1	1*
Springside	2	1	1	1	1**
Spruce Lake	1	1	1	1	1*
Spy Hill	2	1	1	1	1**
St. Brieux	2	1	1	2	1***
St. Front	1	1	1	1	1*
St. Gregor	2	1	2	1	1***
St. Louis	2	1	1	2	1**
St. Walburg	3	2	3	1	2#
Stalwart	1	1	1	1	1*
Star City	3	2	1	1	1**
Stenen	2	1	1	1	1*
Stewart Valley	2	1	1	1	1*
Stockholm	2	1	1	1	1***
Stornoway	1	1	1	1	1*
Storthoaks	1	1	1	1	1*
Stoughton	3	2	2	2	1***
Stranraer	1	1	1	1	1*
Strasbourg	3	2	2	2	2#
Strongfield	2	1	1	1	1*
Sturgis	3	2	2	1	1***
Success	1	1	1	1	1*
Summerberry	1	1	1	1	1*
Swift Current	5	5	5	5	5
Sylvania	1	1	1	1	1*
Tadmore	1	1	1	1	1*
Tantallon	2	1	1	1	1*
Tessier	1	1	1	1	1*
Theodore	2	2	2	1	1**
Tisdale	4	4	4	4	4
Togo	2	1	1	1	1**
Tompkins	2	1	1	1	1**
Torquay	2	1	1	1	1*
Tramping Lake	2	1	1	1	1**
Tribune	1	1	1	1	1*
Trossachs	1	1	1	1	1*
Tuffnell	1	1	1	1	1*
Tugaske	2	1	1	1	1*
Turtleford	3	2	2	2	2#
Tuxford	1	1	1	1	1**
Tway	1	1	1	1	1*
Tyner	1	1	1	1	1*
Tyvan	1	1	1	1	1*
Unity	4	4	3	3	3
Val Marie	2	1	1	1	1**
Valparaiso	1	1	1	1	1*
Vanguard	3	2	2	1	1**
Vanscoy	1	1	1	1	1**
Vawn	1	1	1	1	1*
Venn	1	1	1	1	1*
Veregin	2	1	1	1	1**
Verwood	1	1	1	1	1*
Vibank	2	2	1	1	1*
Viceroy	2	1	1	1	1*
Victoire	1	1	1	1	1*
Viscount	2	2	1	1	1**
Vonda	2	2	2	1	2#
Wadena	4	4	3	3	2##

1 = MCC; 2 = FCC; 3 = PSC; 4 = CSC; 5 = SWR; 6 = PWR
*** Top 72; **Middle 123; *Smallest 307; ## Top 22; # Smallest 50

Appendix

Appendix, continued					
Community	1961 Cluster	1981 Cluster	1990 Cluster	1995 Cluster	2001 Cluster
Wakaw	3	2	2	2	2#
Waldeck	1	1	1	1	1*
Waldheim	2	2	2	1	1***
Waldron	1	1	1	1	1*
Wapella	3	2	2	1	1**
Waseca	1	1	1	1	1*
Watrous	4	3	3	3	2##
Watson	3	3	3	2	2#
Wawota	3	2	2	2	2#
Webb	1	1	1	1	1*
Weekes	2	1	1	1	1*
Weirdale	1	1	1	1	1*
Weldon	2	1	1	1	1*
Welwyn	2	1	1	1	1**
West Bend	1	1	1	1	1*
Weyburn	5	5	5	5	5
White Bear	1	1	1	1	1*
White Fox	2	1	1	1	1**
Whitewood	3	2	3	2	2#
Wilcox	1	1	1	1	1**
Wilkie	4	3	2	2	2#
Willmar	1	1	1	1	1*
Willow Bunch	3	2	2	1	1**
Willowbrook	1	1	1	1	1*
Windthorst	2	2	1	1	1**
Wiseton	2	1	1	1	1*
Wishart	2	1	2	1	1**
Wolseley	3	2	2	2	2#
Wood Mountain	2	1	1	1	1*
Woodrow	1	1	1	1	1*
Wroxton	1	1	1	1	1*
Wymark	1	1	1	1	1*
Wynyard	4	4	3	3	2##
Yellow Creek	2	1	1	1	1**
Yellow Grass	2	1	1	1	1**
Yorkton	5	5	5	5	5
Young	2	1	1	1	1**
Zealandia	1	1	1	1	1*
Zelma	1	1	1	1	1*
Zenon Park	3	2	1	1	1**

1 = MCC; 2 = FCC; 3 = PSC; 4 = CSC; 5 = SWR; 6 = PWR
*** Top 72; **Middle 123; *Smallest 307; ## Top 22; # Smallest 50

INDEX

Access Telecommunications, 45
ADD Boards, 49
Agricultural industry, 2–3, 21

Battleford Cable, 45
Bedroom communities, 22–23, 34
Business development, methods of, 49

Canada Mortgage and Housing Corporation, 51
Canadian Wheat Board, 2
Central Place Theory, 5, 7–8, 11
Central places
  demand thresholds of, 5–6, 63
  range in, 5
Centres, spacing of, 5–6
Cluster analysis, 11, 19, 21–22, 27, 39, 57
Communications technology, 43, 65
  See also Technologies
  See also Telecommunications technology
Community development initiatives, 50
  See also Economic development
Community economic development, See Economic development
Community Futures, 49
Commuting patterns, 40–42, 57
Consolidated Census Subdivision, 57
Crow Rate, 3
Crow's Nest Pass Agreement, 1

Economic development, 29, 31, 36, 48–49, 61, 64
  impact analysis in, 29, 31–32
  impact assessments in, 29
  and leakages, 30, 37
  and manufacturing, 34
  See also Manufacturing employment and mining, 34
  See also Mining employment
Economic expansion, 19, 53, 64
Employment income, nonfarm, 55

Farm families, 3, 51, 55, 64

Farm incomes, 3, 60
Free trade, 4, 60
FTA, 4
Functional economic areas (FEA), 55–61

GATT, 3–4
Grain markets, international, 3

Health Insurance Registration File, 10
Covered Population data, 10
Highway improvements
  and economic activity, 43
  See also Infrastructure, highways
Housing
  in rural communities, 51, 64
  See also Infrastructure, housing
Hudson's Bay Company, 1

Infrastructure, 18–19, 23, 32–33, 39, 60
  and economic growth, 42–43, 53, 64–65
  electricity and gas, 46, 51
  erosion of, 4, 60–61, 64
  highways, 42–44, 50
  housing, 39, 51, 53, 64
  sewers, 42, 47, 51
  telecommunications, 42–43, 45–46, 51, 53
  transportation, 44, 51, 53
  water, 42, 46, 51
IPSCO steel plant, 46

Kalium potash mine, 46

Labour commutes, 58–60
Labour market areas (LMA), 56–58

Manufacturing communities, 35, 50
Manufacturing employment, 34–35, 37, 39, 53
Manufacturing firms, 15, 17–18, 31–32, 34, 50, 63–64
Mining communities, 33–34
Mining employment, 32–33, 39

Mining firms, 32, 34
Multipliers, 30, 60
Multiplier analysis, 30, 39
Multiplier effects, 31, 36

NAFTA, 4
Natural gas pipelines, 46

Person Registry System, 10
Population density, 6, 50, 59

Regional Economic Development Authorities, 49
Retail market areas, 56
Retail trade areas, 56, 58
Rural Development Corporations, 49
Rural economy, 60
Rural Municipalities (RM), 57–59

Saskatchewan Department of Education, 2
Saskatchewan Department of Highways, 2
Saskatchewan Environment and Resource Management (SERM), 47–48
Saskatchewan Health, 10
Saskatchewan Housing Corporation, 51
SaskEnergy, 46
SaskPower, 46
SaskTel, 2, 45
SaskWater, 46–47
Sewage systems, 47
   and solid waste disposal, 48
   See also Infrastructure, sewers
Shaw Cable, 45
Shopping patterns, 3, 33, 56, 60

Technologies
   adoption of, 2, 55, 65
   capital for labour, 21
   and communications, 2
   improvements in, 60
   in intercity road network, 2
   and transportation, 2, 8
Telecommunications technology, 45–46
   See also Infrastructure, telecommunications
Telecommuters, 43
Trade centre classification, 14, 36
Trade centre hierarchy, 9, 11, 14–15, 17–19, 22, 30–31, 34, 39, 41, 53, 56–57, 63
   Complete Shopping Centre (CSC), 11, 13–15, 18, 22–23, 30–31, 35–36, 41, 44–45, 48, 50–53, 56, 60
   Full Convenience Centre (FCC), 11, 13–15, 17–19, 21–23, 25, 27–28, 30–31, 33–35, 37, 39–42, 44, 48, 50–53, 56, 63–64
   Minimum Convenience Centre (MCC), 11, 13–15, 18, 22–23, 25–26, 30–31, 33–35, 37, 56
   Partial Shopping Centre (PSC), 11, 13–15, 17–19, 21–22, 28, 30–31, 33–36, 41–42, 44, 47, 50–53, 56–57, 63–64
   Primary Wholesale-Retail (PWR), 11, 13–15, 18, 22, 30–31, 41–42, 44–48, 51–52, 53, 56, 60, 63
   Secondary Wholesale-Retail (SWR), 11, 13–15, 18, 22, 30–32, 41–42, 44–48, 50–53, 56, 60, 63
Trade centre network, 18, 23, 31, 37
Trade centre status (community), 32–37, 40
Trade centre system, 3–4, 7–9, 18–19, 25, 30, 36, 40, 50, 63–64
Transportation systems, 6-7, 36, 50, 59
   See also Infrastructure, transportation
   See also Technologies, transportation

Wal-Mart, 53, 56
Water, 46
Water quality, 47
World Trade Organization, 4